ROCK DRAWINGS
OF THE
COSO RANGE
Inyo County, California

an ancient
sheep-hunting cult
pictured in desert
rock carvings

with a foreword by
julian h. steward

publication 4
maturango museum
ridgecrest, california
1987

ROCK DRAWINGS OF THE COSO RANGE
Inyo County, California

CAMPBELL GRANT

SPECIAL APPENDIXES BY
James W. Baird and J. Kenneth Pringle

MATURANGO MUSEUM

Museum Director .... Patricia Brown-Berry, Ph.D.
Curator .... Elva Younkin

Set up and published at the Maturango Press for the MATURANGO MUSEUM of Indian Wells Valley, Ridgecrest, CA. C. E. Van Hagan, *Supervising Editor*.

First printing, January 1969
Second printing, September 1969
Third printing, July 1971
Fourth printing, December 1973
Fifth printing, November 1978
Sixth printing, September 1987

Coordinating Editor, Chet Creider, Jr.

Cover design and title page by Campbell Grant.

MATURANGO MUSEUM PUBLICATION NO. 4

Library of Congress Catalog Card No. 68-58316

ISBN 0-943041-00-7

MATURANGO
PRESS

Yet also we keep the seasons of the sheep,
moving into the desert
toward perpetual summer—
the high-climbing ones
with their horns curving
towards those long dead
long dust.

O sky, we say, upstanding father,
some speech must we offer;
this tight stone shall carry our voice.
And we harrow into it
the shapes of the spirit, the tall ones
whose heads shall mirror the great sun
at his clearest hour
upon our questions.
To this end
we have placed them in the high places,
watching
confronting the wind.

From *The Shaman at Ending*
By Gordon Grant

FOREWORD
by Julian H. Steward

The Great Basin and Colorado Plateau contain thousands of sites of rock art, especially of petroglyphs or pecked figures; yet few of them have been related to the prehistoric cultures excavated by dirt archaeologists. Some petroglyphs of the Colorado Plateau have been traced to the early Anasazi of pre-A.D. 1200, but those of the Great Basin seem almost to have been made by people who left no other remains, although Heizer and Baumhoff have dated certain elements and styles from periods probably spanning several thousand years rather than from a single period or from recent times. In the present volume, Campbell Grant, and James Baird and Kenneth Pringle, his collaborators, have made a major contribution in relating the rock art to archaeology. They have not solved all the problems, but they have built on what little is known—archaeology is fairly recent in this area—and imaginatively advanced a few steps toward the answers.

Perhaps a certain freshness in their approach results from the authors not having been trained archaeologists, for rock pictures disclose much that will never be found in the ground. Campbell Grant, an artist, became interested in rock art only about 1960, but he has already published two superb books: *The Rock Art of the Chumash* in 1965, which deals with the remarkably elaborate polychrome paintings made by the Indians who occupied the Santa Barbara area of California at the coming of the Spaniards and contains many new sites discovered by himself, and *The Rock Art of the American Indian* in 1967, which is by far the most readable and authoritative work on the general subject. In addition, he has published more than half a dozen articles, and, with his present co-authors, is presently engaged in excavations in the Coso Range. James Baird and Kenneth Pringle are geologists and physicists employed by the Naval Weapons Center, which embraces the Coso Range where the petroglyphs are found.

The Coso Range seems an improbable place to find such elaborate, distinctive, and abundant art as that presented here. It lies just west of Death Valley, east of the Sierra Nevada Mountains and south of Owens Lake on the fringe of the Great Basin, which consists largely of semi-desert valleys transected by mountain ranges. In historic times these ranges captured enough rainfall to support some big game and a sparse human population, but rarely enough to sustain perennial villages. During the pluvial period at the end of the last Ice Age, many depressions within the Great Basin had contained fresh water lakes, some almost inland seas, such as Lakes Bonneville and Lahontan, but these have evaporated to become extremely briny remnants or mere salt flats. It is difficult to imagine that considerable changes in cultural ecological adaptations were not concomitants of these environmental changes.

The portion of the Coso Range that rises above 6,000 feet into the piñon-juniper zone, where resources were much more abundant than in the lower valleys, is limited in extent, and only a single peak surpasses 8,000 feet. This range cannot compare with the great White-Inyo or Sierra Nevada Mountains, which reach 14,000 feet, or even the Panamint Range, which borders Death Valley to the east. The local canyons and valleys occur in high rolling tablelands that average about 6,000 feet and are relatively temperate in the hottest summers. To the south, the Coso Range drops abruptly 4,000 feet to merge with the hot flatlands of the northern Mojave Desert. The authors report thousands of mountain sheep petroglyphs in the canyons of the Coso Range that, despite the restricted environmental resources today, indicate the former existence of great herds.

In historic times, nearly all of the Great Basin and the Colorado Plateau which extends eastward across the semi-deserts of southern Nevada, Utah, southern Idaho, and Colorado to the Rocky Mountains, had only a sparse population of Shoshonean-speaking Indians. My own fairly extensive study, between thirty and forty years ago, of the Shoshonean Indians disclosed that they knew nothing of the authorship or meaning of the petroglyphs, and that their culture seemed unlikely to manifest itself in this medium.

First, the Basin-Plateau—or "Numic"—division of Shoshonean speakers had the simplest culture in the Western Hemisphere, and in some respects in the entire world. This alone does not prove that they made no petroglyphs, for the Kalahari Bushmen of Africa, the Australian aborigines, and the palaeolithic Europeans had a fairly elaborate rock art. It may be significant, however, that most of these peoples painted their caves and rocks, whereas the Great Basin Indians pecked their petroglyphs on extremely hard basalt or granite cliffs and boulders, which is a major chore. The degree of Shoshonean nomadism seems to me not conducive to such effort. Moreover, none of the various Shoshonean activities or categories of culture, except basketry, were expressed in any art form.

A second argument against recent Shoshonean authorship of the Great Basin petroglyphs, including those of the Coso Range, is that although mountain sheep were the principle subject, these animals are now, as the authors point out, greatly reduced in numbers. Their importance in historic times would hardly inspire the thousands of petroglyphs recorded here.

A further difficulty in attributing the petroglyphs to the modern Indians is that representations of both the atlatl, or spearthrower, and the bow and arrow were portrayed in the Coso Range, but we know that the bow replaced the atlatl in the southwestern United States a century or so after the time of Christ. Also, Heizer and Baumhoff have shown that certain designs had even greater antiquity. Grant and his co-authors quite convincingly suggest that the climax of the Coso Range rock art must have been achieved at a fairly remote time, when the area still supported numerous mountain sheep and yet after the bow, which probably is more effective than the atlatl in hunting these animals, had been introduced and begun to diminish the herds. Their theory that this art was part of hunting magic and that it was placed along game trails is supported by the presence of hunting blinds built of rocks. They also postulate that magic was most likely used in hunting hard-to-get animals and that sheep were being reduced by bow hunting. I suggest also that the climate may have been dessicating at this time following a moister phase that had supported more sheep.

The identity of the early artists still remains in doubt. If the art climaxed at or a few hundred years after the time of Christ, possibly it can be ascribed to the Numic division of Shoshonean, for glottochronology seems to indicate that the three subdivisions of Numic may have originated in this region and begun to differentiate into largely distinctive dialects— Northern Paiute, Shoshoni- Comanche, and Ute- Southern Paiute- Chemehuevi— between 1,000 and 2,000 years ago. Thus the petroglyphs were probably proto-Numic and possibly proto-Shoshonean or even antecedent to any Shoshonean speakers. It is highly improbable that the Western Shoshoni, who occupied the country in historic times, had differentiated from their linguistic kin.

A few petroglyphs, such as bear tracks, may have been made by ancestors of the Western Shoshoni or of the Ute- Southern Paiute- Chemehuevi, who occupied the deserts immediately to their south, but I find it difficult to recognize much in the recent Shoshonean culture or society that might have inspired or even supported the greater part of this art.

In a recent reassessment of the nature of Basin-Plateau Shoshonean society, I recognized that in the arid areas there were no aboriginal bands or social aggregates that numbered more than five closely intermarried families. These small family clusters wintered together, and they wandered during the remainder of the year in search of food, which they shared. They had no ceremonialism, such as the sheep cult suggested by the authors, and they lacked virtually all aesthetic expression. The sheer physical effort and time to peck these pictures would have been excessive, especially since most of the pictures are not now near water, that is, near permanent habitations.

Shoshonean subsistence activities have no apparent relationship to this art. The Indians constantly verged on starvation, and it has always seemed to me that certain crucial plant foods, such as pine nuts, sand bunch grass, or mesquite beans, might have entered their magic and art, but apparently this was not the case. Hunting involved some cooperation between family clusters, as in the case of rabbit or antelope drives, but these were entirely secular. The so-called antelope shaman of many Nevada groups—a man who possessed supernatural power to charm the animals into docility and draw them into a corral—was apparently unknown to the Coso Range Shoshoni. The nearest thing to supernaturalism in hunting was special powers acquired by individuals in dreams, such as ability to run fast, hunt skillfully, or perform other feats. These powers were not portrayed visually, and, despite the constant scarcity of food, there is little evidence of recourse to the supernatural in any subsistence activities. I encountered only one shaman in all Nevada who claimed the ability to make rain. The true shaman usually restricted his activities to curing or otherwise assisting individual persons, and he rarely performed for the benefit of the group.

By stretching the imagination, many cultural objects may be seen in the petroglyphs. Circles might be hoops for the hoop-and-pole game. Some of the so-called "shields" look a little like cradles, although there is no evidence of a human fertility cult. One can see in other figures, possible rabbit nets or tally markers for the many dice games. But it is easier to postulate that most of the petroglyphs, especially the sheep, anthropomorphs, "shields" and "medicine bags," were made by groups of some size with permanent settlements, long ago when sheep flourished locally.

It seems to me that the authors have made a very convincing case, however, for the association of the rock pictures with hunting magic; for the sheer number and the location of mountain sheep petroglyphs as well as remnants of stone blinds leave no alternative explanation that I can think of. This association might, however, have taken several forms: a group ceremony, which could also explain the stick-like dancing human figures, often seeming to bear a burden; an observance at a young man's initiation into hunting, perhaps on the occasion of his first kill; or representation of dreamed powers, a nearly universal North American belief. Perhaps we shall never have the exact answer, but we are learning to ask the right questions.

I strongly doubt that these pictures had any connection with warfare, and the authors use the term "shield" as a means of designating certain designs rather than to imply an interpretation. Although shields have been found in eastern Utah, probably dating from the Anasazi period, the absence of warfare among the Shoshoneans is worth mentioning because so many persons have ascribed them bands which defended their territory, and more recently so much nonsense has been written about mammalian territoriality as the universal basis for warfare. There is no evidence that either bands or competition for territory existed in the Great Basin before the white man arrived.

The interesting conclusion about this rock art is that it signifies culture loss in the area, owing either to deculturation of the present inhabitants or to the earlier presence of a different people. Those who have postulated a Desert Tradition that endured some 10,000 years and was manifest in the recent Shoshonean culture forget that petroglyphs were part of the culture at certain stages and that they represent activities that dirt archaeology will probably never disclose. Magic and ceremonialism in this area is not likely to be identified from objects dug from the ground.

The kind of book that Grant, Baird, and Pringle have given us is to my mind definitely what is needed now. It deals intensively with a delimited region without losing the broader perspective. It is even now being accompanied by excavations. And it does not hesitate to indulge in speculation, which is always necessary: for hypotheses are replaced by better hypotheses, not by so-called "facts."

Julian H. Steward
Department of Anthropology and
Center for Advanced Study
University of Illinois

TABLE OF CONTENTS

Foreword vii

Introduction 1

1. The Country 2

2. Cultural Patterns: Prehistory and History 4

3. The Rock Drawings 12

4. Styles and Subject Matter 16
    Early Period 17
    Transitional Period 17
    Late Period 18

5. Techniques 25

6. Interpretation 29

7. Dating the Rock Drawings 43
    Patina, Erosion, and Lichen Overgrowth 43
    Sequence of Hunting Weapons 48
    Superimposition 56
    Association With Archaeological Materials 56
    Possible Dating of Coso Range Rock Drawings 57

8. The Major Sites 59
    Petroglyph Canyon 59
    Sheep Canyon 70
    Horse Canyon 73
    Renegade Canyon 76

9. The Surrounding Minor Sites 89

10. Relationships With Adjoining Areas 104
    Owens Valley 104
    Death Valley 106
    Walker Pass—Kern River 106
    Northern Mojave Desert—Tehachapi Range 108

11. Conclusions 112

Appendix A
    Methods of Recording 117

Appendix B
    Distribution and Tally of Design Elements 119

Appendix C
    Contact With Other Areas in the West Shown by Design Elements 122

Appendix D
  The Desert Bighorn 125

Appendix E
  The Bighorn Sheep in North American Rock Art 130

Appendix F
  Material Culture Items Shown in Rock Drawings 134

Appendix G
  Geology of the Coso Rock Art Region by J.Kenneth Pringle 135

Appendix H
  Adjacent Occupation Sites by James W. Baird 137

Appendix I
  Update by Author 139

Bibliography 141

Index 145

INTRODUCTION

The Naval Weapons Center (NWC) is located at the northern edge of the Mojave Desert between the Sierra Nevada and the Panamint Range. The Base, with headquarters at China Lake, covers an area of roughly 1,200 square miles of dry lake beds, desert mountains, and volcanic lava flows. It is the Navy's largest ordnance research and development organization. Created in 1943, NWC has grown to a community of over 12,000 persons and has developed many important weapons, especially in the guided missile and rocket field.

The northern half of the giant base is the target or impact area for the missile testing, and it is in the center of this area that the great concentrations of rock drawings are found. Fragments of missiles and the wrecks of drone planes, evidence of two decades of ordnance testing, lie scattered near the basalt cliffs, and pecked on these cliffs are drawings of ancient man hunting the bighorn sheep with weapons of *his* time, the spearthrower or atlatl and the bow and arrow.

The survey of these sites was begun in September 1966 by Campbell Grant, James W. Baird, and J. Kenneth Pringle, supported by a research grant from the Wenner Gren Foundation for Anthropological Research, and continued through October 1967. The cave excavation in Upper Renegade Canyon was made possible through the generosity of Mrs. Albert B. Ruddock, Mr. Harold S. Gladwin, and Dr. John E. Cushing.

We are most grateful to the Naval Command at China Lake for making available equipment and services, and to the Desert Motors Ford agency of Ridgecrest for supplying a Bronco four-wheel drive vehicle for the explorations.

We are much indebted to Dr. Julian H. Steward, Dr. Robert F. Heizer, and Harold S. Gladwin for their reading of the manuscript and helpful suggestions, to Ralph and Florence Welles for their expert assistance on the Bighorn Sheep section, and to Don Martin, longtime rock art student, for his many suggestions on the survey and help on the Death Valley section.

Our thanks to Henry Wittenmyer, Tom and Diane Jones, Haven Silver, Tony Reitz, Gordon Grant, Donald Martin, John Parrish, Dean Blanchard, and Marshall Bond who helped us locate the sites and especially to John Cawley for his enthusiasm and companionship during our Coso trips, and Tony Rose who took many of the photographs.

And finally our gratitude to Kenneth H. Robinson of the Maturango Museum who coordinated all our efforts to produce the finished report.

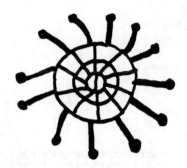

1. THE COUNTRY

The historic territory of the Western Shoshoni in California has probably more geographic variety than any other region of comparable size in North America. Stretching from the Sierra Nevada crest, west of Olancha and Little Lake, the boundary runs northeast along the southern edge of Owens Lake; north along the eastern slope of the Inyo Range; then northeast to include the Saline and Eureka Valleys. To the south, the territory includes Indian Wells Valley and the northern sections of Panamint and Death Valleys. This region of southeastern California is part of the Great Basin. The streams all flow into shallow lakes or are dissipated in the desert sand. Its life zones range from the Lower Sonoran Zone in Death Valley with points below sea level, to the Boreal Zone in the Panamint and Sierra Nevada Mountains with peaks over 12,000 feet. The high country in the Sierra Nevada can have 60 to 70 inches of precipitation (mostly in the form of snow), while the lower desert basins average two inches or less. The winter storms, moving south and east, invariably release most of their rain in the Sierra Nevada, with little left over for the desert ranges farther east. The desert valleys have tremendous temperature ranges. In Death Valley summer temperatures can reach 134°F. and in the winter fall as low as -30°F. near the mountain tops.

The region that will concern us in this report is the Coso Range bounded on the west by the Sierra Nevada, on the north by Owens Lake, on the east by the Argus Range, and on the south by Indian Wells Valley. The highest point is Coso Peak (8,160 feet), with an average annual rainfall of 20 inches—enough to maintain a number of springs, mainly on the southeastern slopes of the mountain. Southwest of Coso Peak there is evidence of much volcanic activity, both ancient and recent. The basically granitic rock structure has been ruptured by numerous cinder cones, and immense basaltic flows have been extruded and then faulted, forming the cliffs of smooth volcanic rock used by the prehistoric people of the area for their rock drawings. These old malpais formations have been much fractured and tremendous blocks of basalt lie tumbled at the base of the canyon walls.

The name "Coso" comes from a Shoshonean word for fire. It seems likely this referred to the abundant evidence of volcanic activity. The fumaroles, or volcanic vents, at Coso Hot Springs continue to send out hot vapours at temperatures of at least 204°F. Before the closure of the area by the Navy Base, the hot springs were popular among Indians as well as whites.

Some characteristic plants of the Coso Range are sagebrush (*Artemisia tridentata*), rabbitbrush (*Chrysothamnus teretifolius*), creosote bush (*Larrea tridentata*), Mexican tea (*Ephedra sp.*), and at the higher levels, Joshua or tree yucca (*Yucca brevifolia*), juniper (*Juniperus californica*), and the single-leaf piñon (*Pinus monophylla*). Water-loving willows are found only in the immediate vicinity of springs.

Upper Petroglyph Canyon, Looking Toward (P-4) From (P-9).

Prominent among the animals of the Coso Range are the blacktailed jack rabbit, desert cottontail, bobcat, coyote, badger, and Inyo mule deer. The magnificent bighorn sheep (*Ovis canadensis nelsoni*), long thought to have become extinct in the area along with the pronghorn antelope, has been reported recently by Fish and Game officials in the adjacent Argus Range.

The entire Coso Range is within the boundaries of the big Naval Weapons Center, and for nearly 20 years it has been closed to all hunting. Recently the regulations have been relaxed to permit a few weekends of hunting every year for rabbits, quail, and chukar. The chukar, an introduced game bird, has multiplied tremendously on the Base and today is the most abundant bird of the region. Hundreds of wild burros share the high mesas with small bands of wild horses.

2. CULTURAL PATTERNS: PREHISTORY AND HISTORY

The last of the great rainy periods or pluvials occurred during the latter half of the Wisconsin Glaciation and lasted until about 10,000 years ago (Sayles and Antes 1941). This was the Provo or "Great Pluvial." The constant rains of this period formed a series of large lakes in four basins of eastern California. The first of these was Owens Lake, between the Sierra Nevada and the Inyo Mountains. As this lake filled, it spilled over its southern brink, sending a stream of water flooding into China Lake Basin and Searles

Water-worn Basaltic Rocks Just Above Fossil Falls.

Basin to create Searles Lake. The pluvial river created by the overflow from Owens Lake eventually cut a deep channel through the lava bed above Little Lake and formed a 40-foot water-fall. Today it is known as the Fossil Falls, and the dark lava still holds the fantastic shapes carved into it by the ancient river. Searles Lake, over 600 feet deep at its maximum, overflowed to the east and north to form another lake in the Panamint Valley

Trough. Panamint Lake, nine hundred feet deep and over sixty miles long, sent its excess water through Wingate Pass into Death Valley, where it combined with water from the Mojave and Amargosa River drainages to form Manley Lake, the last of this chain of prehistoric lakes. (Manley and Panamint Lakes had completely dried up by the beginning of the historic period, but Owens Lake, fed by Owens River, lasted until the 1920's when the river was diverted into the Los Angeles aqueduct system. A vestige of ancient Searles Lake still exists near Trona.).

There is no doubt that early man was living in the area when these lakes still held considerable water. The Pinto site at Little Lake was occupied at a time when a sizeable stream was running through the Little Lake Narrows into the China Lake Basin (Harrington, 1957).

It must have been a region of ample vegetation where nothing but hardy desert plants are found today. Many animals now extinct still roamed the area. Between 9,000 and 7,000

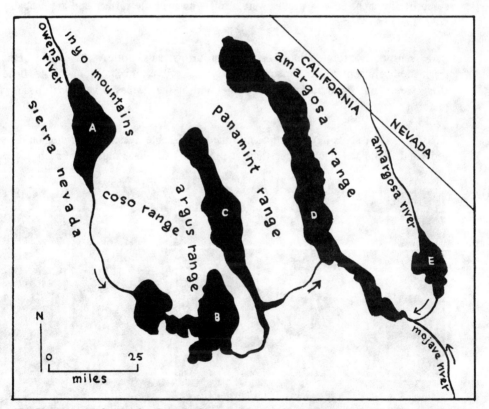

The Pleistocene Lakes in the Coso Region. A. Owens Lake; B. Searles Lake; C. Panamint Lake; D. Manley Lake; E. Tecopa Lake. (After Snyder, Harman and Zdenek, 1964.)

years ago, the country became progressively dryer and hotter, driving the big game animals to the more and more limited water sources where man was established. As a result of man's hunting and the changing climate, many animals, including the horse, camel, and giant sloth, had disappeared before 6,000 years ago. The climate continued dry and hot until the Altithermal Period, or "Great Drought," was broken by another rainy era, the "Little Pluvial" of 3,000 to 4,000 years ago. It is quite possible that Owens Lake again overflowed through the Little Lake Narrows into the Searles Lake Basin during the "Little Pluvial." It is in relation to this period that we have our first certain knowledge of early man in the Coso region.

In 1948, Mark Harrington and Willy Stahl began excavating a village deposit of the Pinto Basin Culture near Little Lake at the western edge of the Coso Range. The site is on a bench above the long-dry stream bed that once fed the three lower Pleistocene lakes. Little Lake is a spring-fed body of water in a volcanic gorge. Nearly 500 Pinto projectile points, many scrapers, and other chipped implements were found. A few of these were of chalcedony, chert or jasper, but most of the chipped material was of obsidian from the extensive quarry at Sugarloaf Mountain several miles to the northeast. Manos, metates (milling stones), and hammerstones were abundant—made of basalt, the dense volcanic stone of the area. Several pestles were also found near the surface and are probably of later Shoshonean origin.

In a nearby cave formed in a lava outcrop, arrowheads, pottery sherds and basketry fragments were found near the surface, all typical of Western Shoshoni culture. Beneath these were Late Basketmaker atlatl points and at the deepest level, Pinto Basin type material.

Tree holes (soft spots in the hardpan), formed by sizeable trees once standing on the site, indicated a climate much wetter than at present. The village must have been occupied

Little Lake From the Southwest Shore. (Iny-26) in distance across lake.

during the last rainy period, the Little Pluvial. In this same hardpan, Harrington and Stahl found postholes arranged in circles, and ovals where seven huts or shelters of some kind had stood—the oldest known houses in the New World.

On the basis of the material excavated at the Little Lake site, the people who lived there 3000 or more years ago were hunters and seed gatherers. They hunted with the spear-thrower, or atlatl, and their seeds were ground into flour by manos on metates. They prepared their game with knives and scrapers of obsidian and they lived in brush shelters. With the exception of the change from the atlatl to the bow and the addition of some pottery, the Indians in the area when the first white settlers arrived in 1860 were living exactly as did their remote ancestors thousands of years before.

The first white people to travel through the area were the members of the expedition led by Joseph Walker, who had gone west in 1833 to look for new beaver country. He found little beaver, but he and his tough mountain men crossed the Sierra Nevada and wintered in Monterey. The following February with 52 men, 330 horses and 400 cattle, he started east. From the lower San Joaquin Valley, he was guided up the Kern River and over the pass that now bears his name by Chumash Indians who had escaped from the missions near Santa Barbara.

The pass drops directly down into the Little Lake area, but Zenas Leonard, who wrote the only account of the Walker expedition, makes no mention of Indians in this area. Actually, the reputation of these trappers, who had wantonly killed many "Digger" Indians in central Nevada on their way west, had probably caused the natives along their path to go into hiding.

Typical Bedrock Metate, or Grinding Surface. These occur by the thousands.

The first entry of the Coso Range by whites came in 1860 when Dr. Darwin French, prospecting out of Visalia for the legendary lost Gunsight Mine, found silver ledges there. A brief flurry of mining interest followed, but none of the early strikes proved important.

At about the same time, cattlemen began to enter the Owens Valley to raise beef for the mining camps. Friction with the Indians began and steadily worsened. Most of the trouble concerned the Owens Valley Paiutes, but the Western Shoshoni of the Coso region were inevitably involved as stockmen and miners appropriated their water and shot the local game. By the late 1860's, the Indian wars were over—a few whites had been killed, and many Indians.

The historic Indians of the Great Basin belong to the Plateau or Numic Branch of the Shoshonean linguistic group. At some distant time the Numic Branch became separated from the Takic or southern Californian Shoshoneans, which includes the Gabrielino and the Serrano. According to Lamb (1958), about 2000 years ago or less the Numic speakers separated into three mutually unintelligible but somewhat similar dialects: the Northern Paiute, Shoshoni-Comanche, and the Ute- Southern Paiute -Chemehuevi. These Shoshoneans were part of an even larger group, the Uto-Aztecan language family that included the Hopi, Pima, and the famous Aztecs of Mexico.

Lamb has theorized that about 1000 years ago the Numic Shoshoneans began to migrate from southeastern California and southern Nevada to the east and north until they dominated the Great Basin and the Colorado Plateau. These migrations eventually replaced or absorbed the earlier people they encountered. Such a dating is based on linguistic studies that indicate that this great shift of population must have occurred over a relatively short period of time. The Northern Paiute pushed to the north as far as central Oregon; the Shoshoni migrated to the northeast and into Utah, Idaho and Wyoming (the Comanche of Texas broke away from the Shoshoni of Idaho and Wyoming as recently as 200 years ago after acquiring the horse), and the Ute-Southern Paiute-Chemehuevi moved eastward through Utah into Colorado.

The prehistoric people of the Coso Range were probably Western Shoshoni, speaking a Shoshoni-Comanche dialect, but as all three Numic branches came from virtually the same area and shared a common culture, it is of no great importance.

The main reasons for these migrations were certainly the continual drying up of the country and the disappearance of game animals. The testimony of the rock drawings, as will be discussed later, indicates abundant game and a sizeable population in the Coso region a thousand or so years ago.

The population of this area in historic times was remarkably small. Kroeber (1925) doubted that this barren region would have supported as many as 500 people. An 1883 estimate put the population at 150; in 1891, less than 100; in the 1920's, a little over 100. Steward (1938) received the following census estimates from local Indian informants (estimates are for 1870 period): Saline Valley, 65; Death Valley, 42; Little Lake, 55 or more; Coso Hot Springs, 100 or more.

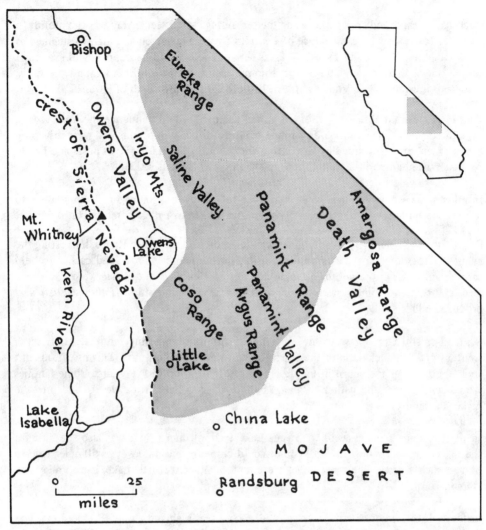

Range of the Western Shoshoni (Shoshoni-Comanche) in California (indicated in grey). (Adapted from Steward, 1938.)

Although this is a very large region, it was only inhabited in a few spots where springs came to the surface. The settlements near the springs were in no sense permanent villages, as the people were constantly on the move, foraging from one food-gathering area to another. The Coso Range is mainly in the Upper Sonoran and Transition zones, and there are a great variety of plants that were harvested seasonally.

The following information about the seasonal activities of the Western Shoshoni of the Coso Range was obtained by Julian Steward in 1935 from Indians who had lived or were still living in the area. The account centers around the Coso Hot Springs village.

In winter, they lived in pit houses, eating stored seeds and hunting rabbits. In April, some families moved to a nearby large spring where they stayed several months gathering greens (such as mustards and cress) and eating the remaining stored seeds. May was the month to go to Owens Lake where the larvae of a certain fly were collected and highly esteemed as food. In June they usually moved to areas where rabbits could be trapped, and if enough people had gathered, they joined for a communal antelope hunt. Antelope were fairly numerous in Indian Wells Valley south of Little Lake and also south of Owens Lake.

The antelope hunt director (who was not a shaman) would announce the hunt several days in advance. The antelope, fast runners but notoriously poor jumpers, were driven by 8 or 10 men, probably aided by fire, into a wide-mouthed corral made of posts and brush. Archers posted around the corral then shot the milling animals inside.

In midsummer some families would make the long trips into Saline or Death Valleys to harvest mesquite seeds. These seeds were ground into flour for easy transportation home.

From July to September, most families wandered through the Coso Range, harvesting the many varieties of seeds that would be stored in the winter village food caches to help carry them through the winter. Several varieties of *Mentzelia* and *Salvia* were important seed plants. Sand bunch grass (*Oryzopsis*) and devil's pincushion (*Echinocactus*) also produced edible seed.

September and October were the most important food gathering months. All families went into the higher parts of the Coso Range to gather piñon nuts. This nutritious nut took the place of the acorn in the desert ranges. If the crop was very large, some families would winter near the gathering area. If the crop was light, trips were made into the higher Panamint Range to the east.

In the fall some families went to Owens Lake to hunt ducks. This was also the time for the big communal rabbit drives. People would come from as far away as 50 miles to take part in such a drive. The main drives were held at Olancha, Little Lake, Rose Valley and Darwin Wash.

In these drives, one or two nets were used, each 2 feet high and about 100 feet long. The net was propped up at intervals with short sticks. With about 10 men beating the bush, the rabbits were driven into the entangling net to be dispatched with clubs by other hunters behind the nets. The flesh was roasted and the skin saved for rabbit-skin blankets.

Hunting by individuals added variety to the diet, but was only incidental to the main food gathering pattern. Mountain sheep and deer were hunted in the Inyo Range and in the Sierra Nevada.

The only communal event not associated with hunting or food gathering was the fall festival. Following the piñon nut harvest and the rabbit hunts, large numbers of people would gather at Coso Hot Springs, Olancha, Saline Valley or Northern Death Valley to gamble, dance the circle dance and observe the annual mourning ceremonies. In this dance, men and women joined hands and moved slowly around in a circle, facing the center, keeping time to songs. It was thought to bring general well-being and was identical to the Paiute-instigated Ghost dance that swept through the western tribes from 1888 to 1891.

A House Ring at Iny-38.

The Western Shoshoni had certain cultural ties with the Indians of the San Joaquin Valley and southern California such as the ceremonial skirt of strings of eagle down and feather quill headbands. Their basketry has an affinity with that of the Yokuts. They made the conical seed-gathering basket, seed-beaters, narrow-necked water bottles pitched on the inside, and the carrying cap worn by women. They had some fair pottery, grey-brown on the outside and black inside. The Western Shoshoni bow was of mesquite or willow backed with sinew.

This is about all we know of the Coso Indians. Their possessions were meager, amounting in effect to a survival kit. That it was efficient was demonstrated by the continued existence of these people in a harsh and unproductive country. The endless search for food left little time for an art form, other than basket designs to develop, and these People had none. It had not always been so. For a very long time their ancestors practiced the art of drawing on stone and became highly proficient, but by the time the white man got around to asking about these rock drawings, not even the oldest Indian could give the slightest information—only that they had been done long ago by the ancients for an unknown purpose.

3. THE ROCK DRAWINGS

On the basalt cliffs of the Coso Range and wherever smooth volcanic rocks occur near springs, there are many thousands of prehistoric rock drawings. These are pecked into the brown-black patina of the stone surfaces and many remain surprisingly fresh-looking, though the most recent must be at least several hundred years old.

The sheer number of these pictures is astonishing. The present investigation has demonstrated that there is no other comparable concentration of petroglyphs in North America. The sites are generally scattered through the mountains, but the climax area lies in two canyons south of Coso Peak where the average elevation is 5000 feet.

The first, Petroglyph Canyon, rises to the northwest of Louisiana Butte (6876 feet) and runs in a southwesterly direction to China Lake Basin. About four miles east and parallel to Petroglyph Canyon is Renegade Canyon. It rises to the east of Louisiana Butte, cuts through Wild Horse Mesa, and terminates at China Lake Basin. Petroglyph Canyon is called Black Canyon in some early records and later, Big Petroglyph. Other names for Renegade Canyon are Sand Tanks and Little Petroglyph. In some of the narrower stretches of Renegade Canyon, basins have been worn into the solid rock streambed. These are filled with sand deposited by storm runoff, which retards the evaporation of trapped water. Animals, particularly coyotes and wild burros, dig down through the sand to water during the summer months—hence the name, Sand Tanks. To avoid confusion, we have kept the most widely accepted names that appear on all maps and records—Petroglyph and Renegade.

The Sand Tank Section of Renegade Canyon Shortly After a Rain.

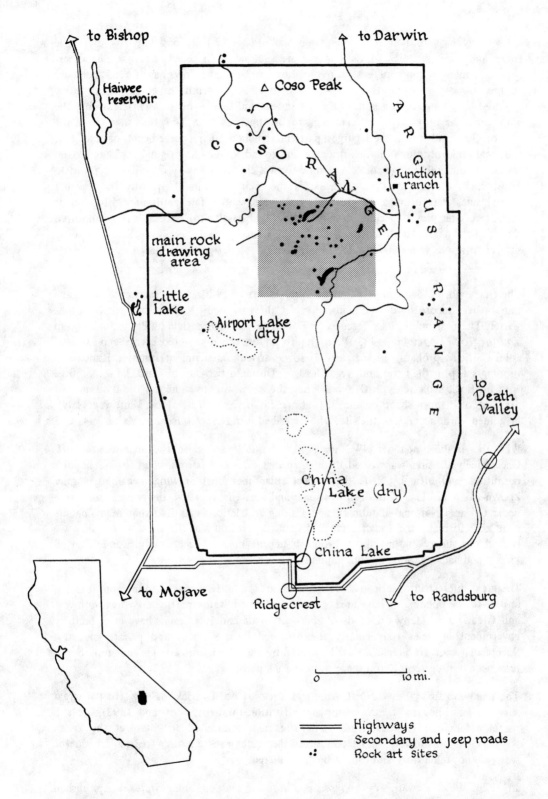

The Naval Weapons Center, China Lake. The shaded area corresponds to the map on p. 59.

These canyons and their tributaries (see map on page 13) are basically of old granitic rocks and through much of their length are shallow drainage ways across high desert mesas. In many sections of both canyons, however, old lava flows have forced their way to the surface, subsequently block-faulting to create intermittent gorges, some a few hundred feet long, others continuing for several miles. The malpais cliffs forming the gorges may be only 20 or 30 feet high, or as much as 400. They rise sheer from the canyon floor and it is in these gorges, particularly where such a gorge begins or ends, that the great concentrations of rock drawings are found. Often the original cliff has broken up into innumerable huge rocks that now form a chaotic stairway from base to rimrock. These rocks offered multiple surfaces for the rock artist and frequently the top and several sides were utilized. Where the gorges narrow to a few yards in width, ancient torrents of the pluvial periods have worn the hard basalt into smooth water-sculptured shapes. In the area with the earliest drawings, many were deeply pecked into rocks subject to severe water erosion. In the later periods all designs were placed well above the highest flood line.

The first reported description of these canyons was in 1929 when a section of Renegade Canyon was recorded for the University of California by F. R. Johnson and Robert A. Carter. The first published reference on Renegade was in an article by Philip Johnston in *Touring Topics*, October 1933. Petroglyph Canyon was discovered by a sheep rancher, John Carricut, probably in the early 1920's. Carricut was living at Junction Ranch and running sheep in the Coso and Argus Ranges. During a two-day blizzard, he took refuge with his flock in Petroglyph Canyon. When the storm was over, he saw the thousands of drawings of bighorn sheep on the cliffs above the survivors of his flock. Many years later, he guided Vernon Smith to the site, who described it in *Desert Magazine*, March 1944.

With the establishment of NWC in 1943, all public access to the area was cut off. Occasionally the area was visited through special week-end permit when firing schedules permitted, and little by little these spectacular aboriginal drawings became generally known to archaeologists, both professional and amateur. In 1964, the two canyons were dedicated as a National Landmark and visiting restrictions eased so that many people were able to make the rough drive and spend a few hours at the sites. At the time we started our survey in the fall of 1966, about one mile of each canyon was fairly well known and had been much photographed.

The great interest in American aboriginal rock art is a fairly recent phenomenon. It is due in part to the opening of large areas of western United States, particularly the Southwest and Great Basin. Many hundreds of miles of roads and jeep tracks have been built by government agencies (particularly the National Park Service) and private industry. Spectacular rock art sites can now be visited by car. Numerous articles and some books have been written recently on these western rock pictures.

The man who first studied North American rock art was Garrick Mallery. His two great surveys, published by the Smithsonian Institution (Mallery, 1886 and 1893), are still useful references. He described many sites and attempted to interpret the "rock writings." Unfortunately, most American aboriginal rock pictures—particularly in the west—do not tell a story and cannot be "deciphered."

In 1929, Julian Steward's *Petroglyphs of California and Adjoining States* was published and became a model for many later publications. He was the first to classify design elements and their geographic distribution. Steward and most of the later investigators, however, made only general inferences on interpretation.

The first attempt to tackle the problem from every angle was made by Heizer and Baumhoff (1962). Their study of the curiously aimless-looking rock drawings of Nevada is thorough and their main conclusion, backed by very persuasive evidence, is that most of them were made in connection with hunting magic.

Our study of the Coso Range petroglyphs had two phases. The first involved extensive field work. The topographic maps showed that only a small part of each main canyon had been recorded and that Petroglyph Canyon had a number of very large side canyons about which nothing was known. One such lateral was more than 8 miles long, and produced nearly 3,000 new drawings. On the map we have called it Sheep Canyon. In all, we covered nearly 30 miles of canyons and recorded 14,084 drawings. Wherever drawings were found, all design elements were classified and counted. Many minor sites in the Coso Range were recorded and designs classified, but no exact count was made.

The second phase was the analysis of the vast amount of data collected. The various styles and techniques were defined by the many hundreds of photographs taken at the sites. The styles, techniques, and design elements, when related to superimposition and differential patination, gave us the relative chronology. Interpretations of the meaning or purpose of the petroglyphs were drawn from a study of the cultural history of the region, the archaeological material recovered in the canyons, and from the occupation caves and the subject matter of the rock drawings.

Crossing the Wash Leading to Iny-39. Nearly all sites call for four-wheel drive travel.

4. STYLES AND SUBJECT MATTER

Style refers to the manner in which the artist visualized his subject. Technique is the method he employed in applying this subject to the rock surface.

In the Coso region, the rock drawings fall into four recognizable styles: naturalistic, stylized, abstract, and pit-and-groove.

Naturalistic ....,... Realistic or representational.

Stylized .... Realistic subjects, simplified or conventionalized, but still easily recognizable.

Abstract .... Having little or no reference to the appearance of objects in nature, often decorative patterns. In relation to rock drawings, the term abstract is somewhat misleading. There is no doubt that many seemingly abstract symbols, incomprehensible to us, represented actual objects or ideas.

Pit-and-Groove ..... This style in the Coso Range consists of small hemispheric pits from 1 to 2 inches in diameter and from about 1/2 to 1 inch deep, arranged in lines or at random.

In certain areas of North America, aboriginal rock art has shown a clear transition from naturalistic to stylized, and often the stylization is carried to the point of pure abstraction. This is likely to happen where a nomadic people with a tradition of naturalistic game animal rock drawings adopts a sedentary or semisedentary way of life with the consequent leisure to develop elaborate ceremony and ritual involving the picturing of supernatural beings and forces. An example of this is shown by the Navajo, who gave up their ancient hunting way of life after contact with the higher culture of the Pueblos and rapidly acquired complex religious ideas. The rock drawings of their new deities, closely patterned after the Pueblo kachinas, eventually led to the superb stylized and abstract figures of the Navajo sand paintings.

In other areas, movements of peoples or strong new cultural contacts can often be detected by the superimposition of a naturalistic form of drawing over an earlier stylized design or carefully rendered abstract forms placed over crudely executed animal or human shapes.

In the Coso region, no such obvious change of style can be seen. The drawings in this country cover a very long time span and for the whole period the art tradition remained remarkably stable. We are certain that they are the work of the same people. The style and subject matter of these petroglyphs vary but slightly from early to late. Some new elements appear and others disappear, realistic concepts become stylized and quality of execution improves, but at all times, naturalistic, stylized and abstract drawings appear together. For convenience, we have divided the chronology of the drawings into Early, Transitional, and Late, based chiefly on subject matter, relative patination, and erosion.

EARLY PERIOD

In this period, the only naturalistic drawings are of sheep. They are rather poorly done; the horns are invariably side-view and often hoofs are attempted. Many stylized atlatls, drawn vertically with hook end up, feature greatly exaggerated stone weights. Most of these are of Type 1 (see figure on page 49), but all three types occur during the Early Period. The atlatls usually are found singly or in groups apart from other elements. The only other style that appears on these atlatl panels with any frequency is the abstract. Rarely are the atlatls associated with square-bodied anthropomorphs, sheep and sheep heads. These latter are invariably drawn head-on and highly simplified though there are examples where some realism has been attempted. These symbols are usually arranged in vertical or horizontal rows. One rock has 82 of these horns in a series of vertical rows. The only other stylized figure from this period is the square-bodied anthropomorph (with solidly rendered body, and often phallic).

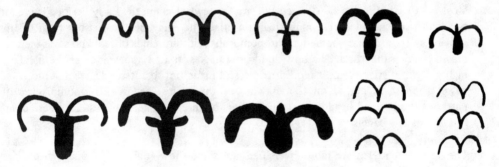

Variations of the Sheep Horn Motif.

There are many abstract patterns from the Early Period and some look older than the earliest atlatls. They suggest an affinity with the Great Basin Curvilinear and Rectilinear styles (Heizer and Baumhoff, 1962; von Werlhof, 1966). Grids, meandering lines, and bisected circles are some of the typical elements, and they are often deeply pecked.

Pit-and-Groove style petroglyphs occur sparingly at the head of Renegade Canyon in association with the deeply pecked abstract and may be very old. Heizer and Baumhoff (1962) place this style as the earliest in the Great Basin (possibly as early as 4000 B.C.).

TRANSITIONAL PERIOD

During this period (marked by the shift from atlatl to bow and arrow), many new subjects appeared on the canyon walls. Some daring artist had given the old naturalistic sheep formula a new twist—horns were attempted head-on and a tradition was established that would eventually become the dominant type. This method of drawing the horns (often with ears added) is probably the most characteristic feature of the Coso sheep. Both these features are extremely rare in other parts of the west. A few isolated examples in Texas may be laid to independent invention, but a single example in Nevada east of the Sierra Nevada and numbers of horns-front sheep from the middle Columbia near Vantage suggest a northern extension of Coso ideas. The early attempts to portray hoofs were abandoned, and body shapes vary from round to square. The number of sheep drawn during this period is prodigious—single rocks will have 50 or more. Long-tailed, short-legged animals frequently appear on panels with sheep and are doubtless dogs used in driving the sheep past the hunting blinds. Scattered through the panels of this period are a few deer.

A curious design first occurs during the Transitional Period (see page 36). It often looks like a fringed sack with a handle and we have called it a medicine bag. It may be just that, though without an actual specimen, it cannot be proven. All other naturalistic drawings are connected in some way with hunting, and this may have been an important object in the hunt ceremonies. The last new realistic element is the projectile and foreshaft. These are precise silhouettes of atlatl or arrow points bound to a short hardwood foreshaft such as have been found in dry caves in Nevada (see page 37).

Most atlatls continue to be stylized but are far fewer than in the Early Period. There are two or three examples of a more realistic atlatl that may be the last drawings of this ancient weapon. Square-bodied anthropomorphs without hands or feet and stick-men are drawn holding the atlatl. The bow and arrow makes its first appearance in the hands of highly stylized stick-men. Sheep horns are still made but to a lesser degree and more and more emphasis is placed on the drawing of the entire sheep. Anthropomorphs with patterned bodies and headdresses, forerunners of the gala figures of the Late Period, are found on a few panels.

The abstract patterns are more diversified and some show considerable imagination. The first "shield" patterns date from this period but are rather simple and poorly executed. The basic size is about one foot square with the design enclosed in a circular, oval or square frame line. The ratio of abstract to naturalistic or stylized is sharply off from the Early Period, reflecting the increasing importance of the sheep cult and the need to actually picture the animal.

LATE PERIOD

The general trend in this final period is toward more stylization and better execution. Sheep, deer, and dogs continue to be drawn naturalistically, though the dog is sometimes pictured with a fantastically long tail, curved over the back and touching the head. Projectiles and foreshafts are rare.

There are many types of stylized sheep, but the dominant style is "boat-shaped" with flat back, round belly, thin legs and tiny head. These are usually done with great care and often life-sized. The tradition of drawing sheep both naturalistic and stylized with horns

Solid body Anthropomorphs, Male and Female. d, (Iny-6); all others, (P-9).

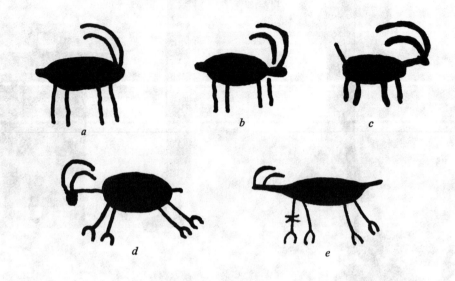

TRANSITIONAL

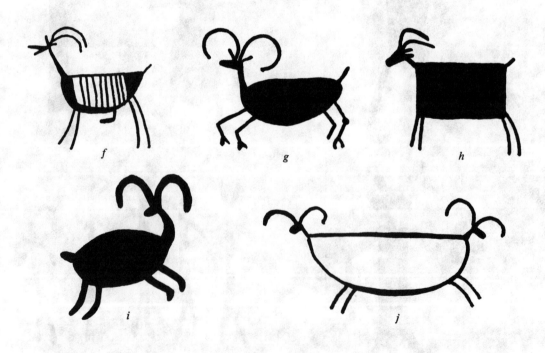

These Two Pages Illustrate the Development of the Sheep Motif in the Coso Region. a, b, and c,

(Iny-34); d, (P-8); e, i, and m, (S-16); f, g, k, p, q, and s, (P-9); h, n, and o, (Iny-5); j, (R-35); l, (S-17); r, (S-20); and t, (Iny-16).

front-view is firmly established as a basic characteristic of the "Coso" sheep. A curious sheep variant of the Transitional and Late Periods is the double-ended or two-headed sheep. There are over 50 examples of this oddity. Another rarer type is the sheep inside the sheep, possibly representing pregnant animals. The solid-body anthropomorphs are often phallic and horned. In only four instances is the subject clearly a woman. There are many examples of processions of stick-figures. They are often shown wearing one or two feathers. The medicine bags are simplified to a geometric shape and become quite decorative. Hunters with bow and arrow are abundant and sometimes are reduced to two vertical lines and one horizontal (see figure on page 54). The arrow is usually shown still attached to the bow and in contact with the sheep, but there are many examples of the sheep impaled with the shaft in the back. This actual picturing of the kill, often associated with attacking dogs, is the first time that such realism was attempted in the Great Basin.

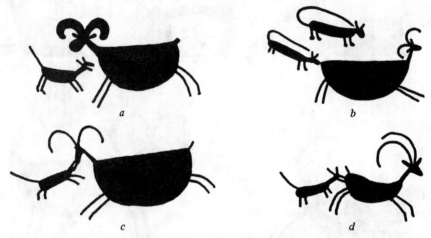

Dogs Attacking Sheep. a and d, (P-9); b, (Iny-5); and c, (S-20).

The most dramatic drawings connected with the Late Period are the elaborate patterned-body anthropomorphs. These figures are about two to three feet high, and feature feathered headdresses, earrings, painted bodies, and fringed skirts. The heads are round balls or concentric circles and features are rarely attempted.

During the Transitional and Late Periods, there are a few snakes, lizards, birds, and animal tracks, all rendered in a conventionalized manner.

The Late Period abstracts are chiefly confined to the handsome shield patterns. We have called them shields for want of a better term, but what they represent or why they were made is unknown. They are the best drawings, technically, that were made in the Coso Range and no two are alike, though similar elements inside the frames appear over and over again in different combinations. Late appearing Pit-and-Groove style petroglyphs found at one spot in Petroglyph Canyon, may be early glyphs retouched.

From the preceding discussion, it is obvious that the Coso rock-drawings pose a real problem for the classifier as all basic styles occur in all three periods. The breakdowns presented in Tables 1 and 2 are about the best that can be made of it (the Transitonal Period is a continuing link between Early and Late Periods).

Shield-like Patterns, Late Period. a through d, and h, (Iny-5); e, f, and g, and i through x, (P-4); and y, (S-17).

23

TABLE 1. Classification of Drawings by Subject Matter in Early, Transitional, and Late Periods

Period	Style	Subject Matter
Early	Naturalistic	Sheep—horns to side—hoofs
	Stylized	Atlatls
		Sheep heads
		Solid-body anthropomorphs
	Abstract	Misc. curvilinear and rectilinear patterns
		Pit-and-groove
Transitional	Naturalistic	Sheep—horns to side and front
		Dogs
		Deer
		Medicine bags
		Projectile foreshafts
	Stylized	Atlatls
		Sheep heads
		Solid-body anthropomorphs and stick-figures
		Patterned-body anthropomorphs (simple)
		Hunters with atlatl
		Hunters with bow
	Abstract	Shield patterns (simple)
		Misc. curvilinear and rectilinear patterns
Late	Naturalistic	Sheep—mainly horns to front
		Dogs
		Deer
	Stylized	Solid-body anthropomorphs
		Processions of stick-figures
		Patterned-body anthropomorphs (elaborate)
		Hunters with bow
		Medicine bags
		Sheep—horns, front only
	Abstract	Shield patterns (elaborate)
		Misc. curvilinear and rectilinear patterns

TABLE 2. Ratio of Naturalistic and Stylized Drawings to Abstract Drawings in Various Locations

Canyon	Period	No. of Drawings	Percentage Naturalistic Stylized	Percentage Abstract
Petroglyph	Transitional and Late	4900	75.90	24.10
Renegade................	Early to Late	6277	67.35	32.65
Sheep	Transitional to Late	2753	89.15	10.85
Horse	Early and Transitional	154	59.60	40.40

5. TECHNIQUES

There are two basic ways of making a drawing on stone. The first is by applying pigment mixed with an oil binder to the rock surface. This technique is confined to areas where the rocks are chiefly light-colored, such as the sandstones and granites. In the Coso Range, there are six sites where some designs are painted, and the style indicates that they are late and done by another group of people. There are single paintings in red or polychrome in red, black, and white.

In the second method, the designs are engraved into the surface of the stone. Volcanic activity in the Coso region has created many miles of malpais (basaltic lava) cliffs that were used as drawing boards by the prehistoric artists. This rock, originally a medium-gray color, has been oxidized to a dark brown or black. The surface is often shiny, hence the term "desert varnish." For a full description of desert varnish, see the section on patination. When the surface of such patinated rocks is shallowly broken with a stone tool, the lighter brownish color of the weathered rock just below the patina stands out in sharp contrast, giving a negative effect of light on dark to the design. Deep pecking through this weathered zone reveals the unaltered rock.

Freshly Fractured Surface Showing Contrast With Patinated Surface (Iny-33).

Over and above this effect, there is another factor that increases the contrast. Many people have noticed how a sharp blow with a hammer on almost any stone surface will produce a lighter spot at the point of impact. This is caused by the shattering of tiny crystals in the rock—the same lighter opaque effect that is seen when glass is splintered with a sharp blow.

The engraving technique can be done in a variety of ways: by incising or cutting into the rock with a sharp rock; by pecking with a pointed stone—either held as a fist-axe or used as a chisel and struck with a hammer-stone; and by abrading—the surface is worn off by scraping with the edge of a stone. All of these techniques and every possible combination of them were employed by the ancient artists.[1]

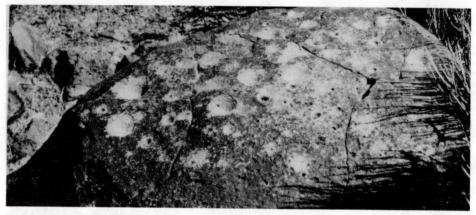

Pit-and-Groove Markings, Deeply Pecked. These appear to be of the Early Period retouched in the Late Period (Iny-33).

The oldest appearing drawings are found in the middle section of Renegade Canyon and feature deep incising or pecking. Some of these designs are made with lines as much as an inch wide and over a half-inch deep. In a few of these, traces of red pigment can still be seen in the deeply incised lines, and it is quite possible that at one time all such drawings were painted. In the entire region, we have recorded only two thin-line scratched panels, one of them with a Type 1 atlatl.

Most of the Coso Range designs were pecked and abraded; sometimes the figures were entirely pecked, but the more usual (and much quicker) method was to outline the design by pecking and scraping off the larger areas, such as a sheep's body, with the abrading stone. The crudest drawings are entirely abraded. The most skillfully executed drawings (and the most recent-appearing) were made by incising the outlines of the figure and then deeply abrading all of the inside areas. This gave a very clean-cut picture (see figure on page 75).

[1] In much of the American literature on rock art, paintings are referred to as pictographs and carvings or engravings are called petroglyphs. Some writers, however, transpose these confusing terms, compounding the confusion and others use petrograph and pictoglyph. For the sake of clarity, we have avoided the lot of them as much as possible and have used the simplest descriptive terms: painting, engraving, pecked drawing, abraded design, etc.

Deeply Incised Grid Pattern in Renegade Canyon. This is the oldest appearing example in the Coso Range.

Sheep Drawings Made by Abrading (R-26).

Scratched Technique in Renegade Canyon (R-25).

Incompletely Pecked Sheep at (Iny-40).

6. INTERPRETATION

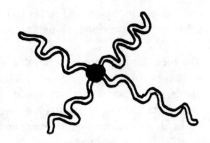

The most difficult aspect of the study of rock drawings is in the field of interpretation—why were they made and what function, if any, did they perform?

There has been a significant upsurge of interest in prehistoric American Indian rock paintings and engravings in the last ten years, and though most of the investigators content themselves with recording and describing sites, a few have made serious attempts to interpret this provocative rock art.

Robert F. Heizer and Martin A. Baumhoff have tackled this phase of the problem in the Great Basin area and their results were published in 1962 (*Prehistoric Rock Art of Nevada and Eastern California*). The characteristic and most widely spread style in the Great Basin is pecked abstract. Heizer and Baumhoff have broken this down into Great Basin Curvilinear Abstract and Great Basin Rectilinear Abstract. Both styles intergrade constantly, though the Curvilinear appears to be the oldest style. To the casual observer, these drawings are the most aimless "doodles"—connected circles, meandering lines, concentric circles, zigzags, and the like. Occasionally recognizable animals, usually sheep, were portrayed.

These investigators visited many sites and studied particularly the environment of each site. Gradually a pattern began to emerge. Almost without exception, the aboriginal rock drawings were located on migratory game trails, near hunting blinds in narrow gorges, or along rock escarpments and in the vicinity of springs where watering animals could be ambushed. Their conclusion was that in some way the rock pictures were connected with the taking of game, that in some ritualistic way the drawings were an aid to hunter success.

Hunting-magic and the picturing of hoped-for game animals on stone have been widely practiced from the earliest times. The superb paintings of extinct animals in the Palaeolithic caves of southern France and northern Spain were doubtless made for this purpose. The Mesolithic paintings of eastern Spain feature the bowmen as well as the game animals. The practice of making such paintings is still carried on in northern and central Australia.

The rock engravings in the Coso Range, particularly in the Petroglyph and Renegade Canyon region, afford ample support for the hunting-magic theory of Heizer and Baumhoff.

These sites at the southwestern edge of the Great Basin differ markedly from the usual haphazard-looking Great Basin style. Here are thousands of mountain sheep, often together with hunters wielding atlatls or bows. Dogs are depicted attacking sheep, bearing out statements by living Paiutes and Shoshoni that in the early days dogs were used to help drive the game animals past ambush points.

The rock drawings are concentrated at four types of localities. Most are at the entrances to gorges containing piled-rock hunting blinds; others are located in conjunction with blinds, on rocky points dominating saddles between watersheds; isolated rocks in the immediate vicinity of springs have engravings, and the rocky crags near Coso and Silver Peaks, have innumerable drawings and many blinds. No drawings were found in canyon areas lacking easy access.

John Muir (1901, pp. 320-322) gives this vivid description of how some Great Basin Indians used the blind in hunting the wary mountain sheep.

> In the more accessible ranges that stretch across the desert regions of western Utah and Nevada, considerable numbers of Indians used to hunt in company like packs of wolves, and being perfectly acquainted with the topography of their hunting grounds, and with the habits and instincts of the game, they were pretty successful. On the tops of nearly every one of the Nevada mountains that I have visited, I found small nestlike enclosures built of stones, in which as I afterwards learned, one or more Indians would lie in wait while their companions scoured the ridges below, knowing that the alarmed sheep would surely run to the summit, and when they could be made to approach with the wind they were shot at short range.

The steep-walled basaltic lava gorges that occur through much of Petroglyph and Renegade Canyons were natural sheep "traps" into which the animals were driven past concealed spearmen or archers. The blinds in the gorges are invariably built slightly above the stream bed so the hunters could shoot down at close range as the sheep ran past. Rock drawings of sheep impaled with arrows or darts always show the projectile striking the middle of the back.

This sort of hunting could only be done communally as large numbers of people were necessary to keep the sheep moving into the gorges and to prevent them from escaping through low points on the canyons. Communal game hunts of this type were important economic ventures and called for the closest coordination by all members of the hunt.

The main hunting areas were in the gorges around Louisiana Butte and Wild Horse Mesa, a region removed by many miles from the springs that are concentrated to the south and east of Coso Peak. That ample water was available in this part of the range that seems so dry today is demonstrated by the innumerable bedrock metates that are found at or near all the rock drawing sites. Actually, rock basins, or *tinajas*, in the canyons trapped and held water from the winter rains for many months. Sand in the basins kept the water beneath from evaporating. During the summers, thundershowers would often refill these natural reservoirs. Many people were involved in the communal hunts, and they had to be fed whether the hunt was successful or not. As late summer and early fall was the time when so many seed-bearing plants were harvested, it seems likely that the main hunts took place at the same period.

Small Hunting Blind Made of Piled Rocks (Iny-42).

The narrow gorges of the Coso Range were ideal for such drives, but in other areas of the Great Basin, corrals were built for the entrapment.

Muir (op. cit.) has described this method:

> Still larger bands of Indians used to make extensive hunts upon some dominant mountain much frequented by the sheep, such as Mount Grant on the Wassuck Range to the west of Walker Lake. On some particular spot, favorably situated with reference to the well-known trails of the sheep, they built a high-walled corral, with long guiding wings diverging from the gateway: and into this enclosure, they sometimes succeeded in driving the noble game. Great numbers of Indians were of course required, more indeed than they could usually muster, counting in squaws, children and all; they were compelled therefore, to build rows of dummy hunters out of stones, along the ridge-tops which they wished to prevent the sheep from crossing. And without discrediting the sagacity of the game, these dummies were found effective; for with a few live Indians moving about excitedly among them, they could hardly be distinguished at a little distance from men, by anyone not in on the secret. The whole ridgetop then seemed to be alive with archers.

In Sheep and Upper Renegade Canyons, such dummy hunters made of piled rocks are located on the edge of the cliffs. They are always on the north facing or shady side of the canyon where they show up only in silhouette from below.

Dummy Hunters Made of Piled Rocks (Iny-8F).

It can never be known exactly how the rock drawings were connected with the hunt. The practice of making such pictures had disappeared long before the first anthropologist began questioning the Indians of the area. According to Driver (1937, p. 86), the Kawaiisu-Ute (who occupied the territory south and southwest of the China Lake region) thought that the drawings were made by a supernatural being; the Western Shoshoni (Coso) stated that they were also made by recent human beings. An Owens Valley Paiute (whose territory adjoined the Western Shoshoni just north of the Coso Range) thought that Paiute of his grandfather's time made rock engravings of supernatural animals and birds and that the goemetric motifs were of an older period (Steward 1933, p. 335).

It is very possible that drawings were made during ceremonies before an important hunt. A communal hunt would be under the direction of an experienced leader such as a local chief. This leader might have made the ceremonial drawings or directed their creation by competent artists. Another possibility would be that the hunters themselves made the drawings. In either case, it was probably believed that the visualization of the quarry would aid in achieving success.

Many rocks are covered with dozens of small sheep drawings. Quite possibly this began when one individual hunter pecked a picture of the animal he hoped to kill. If he was successful, he might think that this particular rock had "power" to bring him good luck, and before another hunt he would again make his drawing on the same rock. Other hunters, noting his success and hoping to acquire some of the rock's power, might have added their pictures.

Certain animals and fish were of great importance to the aborigines of North America as a primary food source. In the Northwest, it was the salmon; on the Great Plains, the buffalo; in the Northern Woodland, the elk and moose; in the Eastern Woodland, the deer; in the western mountains, particularly the Great Basin, it was the sheep. Of all these creatures, the only one widely pictured in rock art is the sheep. At first glance, this seems curious. The sheep, of course, throughout its range, was highly prized for its excellent meat, hide, and horns, and it was hunted by most of the western tribes. The mountain sheep was difficult to capture or kill; easily alarmed, it sought the roughest, most inaccessible country when pursued. We think that the sheep drawings served a ritualistic hunting-magic purpose.

To back up the theory that hunting-magic drawings were *only* employed when the sought-after animal or fish was difficult to obtain, there are the following comparisons. Along the Columbia River where the Indians were almost totally dependent on the seasonal runs of the five species of Pacific salmon, the fish is depicted in only three instances among the many thousands of rock pictures (Emory Strong, long-time student of the Columbia River rock art, personal communication). In the Great Plains, the buffalo seldom appears with other rock drawings, and its casual appearance suggests the plains practice of recording events rather than hunting-magic. In the Northern Woods, elk and moose drawings occur in scattered localities but are never abundant. In the Eastern Woodland, the deer is almost never drawn but indicated by tracks at a number of sites.

The conclusion is inescapable that picture magic was rarely necessary in securing the game animals and fish described above. They were abundant and reasonably easy to catch or kill. Another piece of evidence is that in the Petroglyph and Renegade Canyon drainages we have counted over 7000 drawings of sheep and there are many thousands more if we include all of the Coso Range in the tally. In the same area, the survey has counted only 105 deer and *no* antelope. We have ethnographic evidence that antelope were hunted every year up into historic times in Indian Wells Valley and south of Owens Lake (Steward, 1938). The implication is that hunting magic drawing was rarely used in deer hunting and *never* for the easily procured antelope.

Lhote (1959) describing the magnificent rock paintings in the Tassili area of the Sahara Desert has noted some things about the mouflon, or wild sheep, of north Africa that parallel our findings in the Coso. Pictures of the animal occur in tremendous numbers on the rock walls of the Tassili and through all periods. One wizard was pictured with mouflon feet and wearing the skin of the beast. Sheep horns were painted in scenes suggesting ceremonies. Among the present-day Tuareg the hunter of the mouflon enjoys great prestige due to the difficulty of taking the animal. The hunter of the gazelle, an easy animal to kill, gains no reputation.

Though rock drawings of sheep occur throughout the western states and into Mexico, they are only abundant in three areas: along the Columbia River from Vantage to the Dalles, in the canyons of the Four Corners region of the Southwest, and in the Coso

Range. In this latter region, the numbers are so great that it would be safe to say this one small area (about 250 square miles) contains more bighorn drawings than all the other sheep sites in North America combined.

It is hard to account for such a concentration unless we postulate the gradual development in the Coso region of a sheep cult. Cults (systems of religious belief and worship, especially the rites and ceremonies of such worship) centering around certain animal species are common throughout aboriginal North America. Such animals were believed to have supernatural powers and to be immortal. On the Northwest Coast, the recurrent appearance of the salmon created the belief that the fish ascended the streams to benefit mankind, died, and then returned to life. The salmon were believed to be a race of supernatural beings that lived in a great house under the sea. When the time came for the run, they would assume the appearance of fish to sacrifice themselves.

All the Northwest Coast Indians had many regulations and prohibitions referring to the Salmon-people in order to continue to maintain good relations with these important beings (Drucker, 1963, pp. 154-55). Some Alaskan Eskimos preserve the soul of a whale, seal, or walrus they have killed in a bladder of water. This bladder is kept all winter and early in the spring it is taken to the edge of the sea and the water is poured back into the sea. The soul of the dead animal is told to swim far out where it will find one of its own kind about to be born. Later the souls of the reborn animals are honored at a great ceremony. The Yurok of northwestern California believed that the deer were supernatural people who put on deer shapes and exposed themselves to the hunters who pleased the deer-people. On the plains, supernatural buffalo were the patrons of cult societies who danced in their honor.

The only people who could communicate with these important animal beings were the cult priests or shamans—priests who posed as middlemen between the spirit world and the real world. This rapport was greatly aided by recitations, ritual objects, trances, songs, and ceremonial dancing.

It is likely many of the elaborate drawings of the Transitional and especially the Late Period in the Coso Range were made in relation to a sheep hunting cult similar in intent to the salmon and buffalo motivated cults in the Northwest and on the Great Plains.

The rock drawings in the Coso Range show a development from simple random pictures to elaborate stylizations—a development that may have taken several thousands of years. Glottochronology evidence indicates that this development was carried out by the same people. The most distinctive design elements appear to have originated here—even the method of drawing the bowmen (the bow was introduced into the area *after* the practice of making rock drawings had been established) is peculiar to the region.

The earliest designs seem to be abstract patterns such as gridirons, connected circles, concentric circles, and meandering lines. In this same general period, the first crude sheep drawings occur with stylized atlatls, sheep horns, and simple anthropomorphs. Most of these first drawings are concentrated in Renegade Canyon and indicate a hunting-magic motivation from the earliest times.

The stylized atlatls are almost invariably shown with one, two or three stone weights attached to the weapon. The commonest variety is the type with a single weight. As described in the section on Sequence of Hunting Weapons (page 53), these stones added little to the efficiency of the atlatl and it is likely their chief function was as charmstones or fetishes to bring luck to the hunter.

Primitive people throughout the world have always put great faith in charms and amulets to bring success in undertakings or to protect the wearer against malign forces and dangers. Vestiges of such beliefs have endured among civilized men of the Space Age. Two well-known examples are the rabbit's foot carried for luck and the St. Christopher medals worn by travellers for a safe journey.

Cushing (1883) noted that no Zuni would start on a hunt or expedition without a suitable fetish or charm in his pouch to aid him. These fetishes were usually of stone and carefully finished. The atlatls recovered by Guernsey and Kidder in northeastern Arizona Basketmaker caves had as many as three stones attached. These stones were well shaped and polished and usually placed so close to the finger-grips that they could not possibly have helped balance the weapon. Our experiments demonstrated that additional thrust and force is possible only when the stone is placed toward the distal end of the atlatl.

The Coso atlatl stones are greatly exaggerated in proportion to the size of the weapon. A plausible explanation for this exaggeration is that it might increase the effectiveness of the charmstones if they were depicted as very large. Similar wishful-thinking occurs in many hunting scenes where tiny hunters are shown shooting at huge sheep, proportionately the size of elephants.

Hunters Armed With Atlatls. Such drawings are rare in the Coso Range (P-9).

In the Transitional Period (characterized by the introduction of the bow) some new elements appear that suggest the development of ceremony. The most interesting is what we have called the "medicine bag" (see the figure below). The first ones are quite realistic with fringed base and carrying handle. Hide bags to carry the medicine bundle or collection of the shaman's sacred objects are known from many parts of aboriginal North America. Kirkland and Newcomb (1967) illustrate many examples of the anthropomorphic figures painted on the cave walls of the Lower Pecos River in Texas that are carrying atlatls and fringed pouches. Such pouches or bags have been found scratched on pebbles from Anasazi ruins in southern Nevada. These settlements were abandoned by the Anasazi about A.D. 1150 and occupied by the encroaching Southern Paiute.

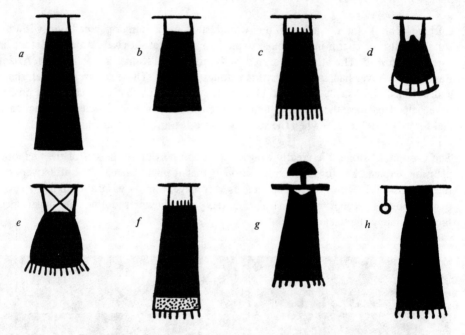

Medicine Bags From Various Sites. A, (S-16); b, c, and d, (P-9); e, (S-16); f, (P-9); g and h, (R-25).

In addition to the solid-body anthropomorphs that continue to be made through all three periods, the rock artists began to make simple patterned-body anthropomorphs that appear to show painted designs on the bodies. Headdresses of various sorts are indicated, both feathered and horned, and often the figures have ear ornaments. These are undoubtedly ceremonial figures, and the accompanying sheep drawings suggest a growing elaboration of rites connected with sheep and sheep hunting. During this period, the simple grid with its enclosing line begins to show a variety of different patterns—patterns that will become increasingly elaborate during the Late Period and that we have called "shields" for want of a more apt description, as they often have a distinct heraldic appearance.

The solid-body anthropomorphs of this middle period are often horned and phallic, and the practice of making them continues down into the Late Period.

 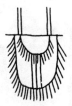

Scratched Designs on Pebbles, Lost City Area, Southeastern Nevada. These suggest the medicine bags from the Coso region. (From specimens in the museum at Overton, Nevada.)

a. Pecked Ceremonial Figure From Sheep Canyon (Iny-9a) With Stylized Weapons (bow and arrow or atlatl and darts). b. Painted Ceremonial Figure From the Lower Pecos River, Texas, With Atlatl, Darts, and Fringed Pouches. (From photograph by David Gebhard).

At a few sites, particularly near Junction Ranch and at Iny-9A, projectile points are featured, and some patterned-body anthropomorphs show such projectile points attached to the shoulders or head, or actually taking the place of the head. This picturing of the spear or arrowhead (with the earlier practice of drawing the atlatl) suggests that the weapons themselves were used in the ceremonies.

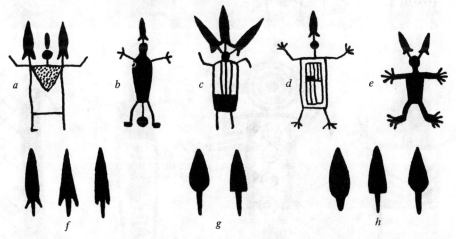

Top. Anthropomorphs With Projectile Points. There are a few examples of this curious combination at four sites. They are of the Transitional Period, and the shape of the points suggests bottom-notched arrow points. a, (R-25); b, (Iny-11); c, (Iny-43); d and e, (Iny-5). Bottom. Projectile Points With Foreshafts. f, (S-15) a Late Period site and probably arrow points; g, (R-35); h, (R-25). These latter groups are Early and Transitional sites and may be atlatl points.

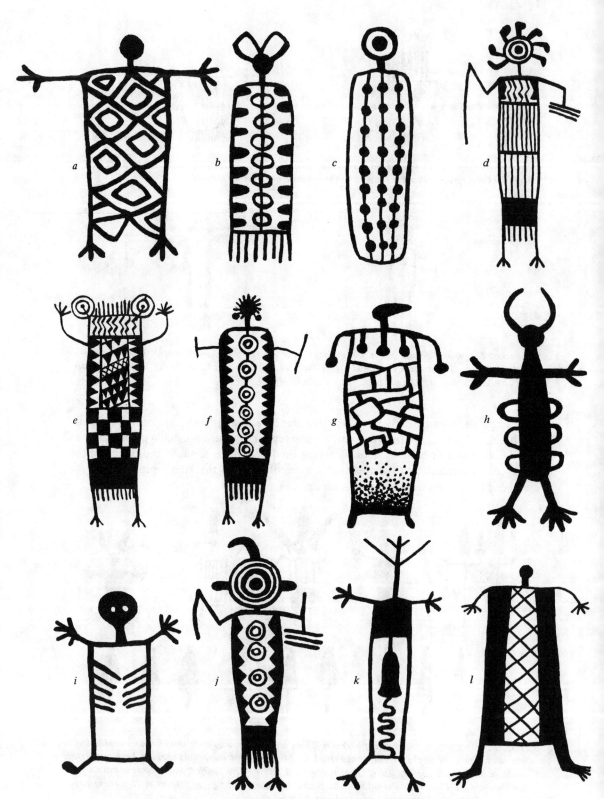

Patterned-body Anthropomorphs of the Transitional and Late Periods. a-f, (R-25); g and h, (R-35); i, (S-16); j-l, (P-9).

The most distinctive additions in the Late Period are the processions of stick-figures (in one instance 86 men are pictured, some carrying large round bundles). These figures are often horned or feathered and certainly tie in with the theory of growing ceremonialism. At the same time, the number of medicine bags increases, and they become highly stylized. The patterned-body anthropomorphs become very elaborate and a basic type occurs again and again, showing fringed skirt, painted body, feathered headdress, earrings, and carrying ceremonial objects. These objects are often a single stick in one hand and three sticks in the other (see the figures on page 38). What they represent, it is impossible to say, though they may symbolize a bow and arrows. These figures almost certainly represent the costumed principals of the sheep cult and may have been the shamans. The shield patterns become standardized to a shape roughly a foot square with an endless variety of interior designs—no two are ever alike. The largest concentration of these is in upper Petroglyph Canyon with the finest examples on the west face. These curious plaques doubtless played an important part in the sheep ceremonies, but one can only guess what it might have been. One possibility is that successful hunters might have been allowed to peck their own personal device or insignia on the rocks in recognition of their feat.

There is a major concentration in Petroglyph Canyon where many thousands of designs are located within a bend in the canyon less than four hundred feet in length. There are 14 examples here where the large, beautifully stylized sheep, so characteristic of the Late Period, are drawn over patterned-body figures, allowing only the head and feet of the latter to show. These sheep are often life-sized and must have taken many hours to execute. Both anthropomorphs and sheep usually appear to be roughly contemporaneous and the only explanation seems to be ritual obliteration. These handsome anthropomorphs are almost without exception placed high on the canyon wall, often just under the rimrock. Such placement may have given the drawings more "power." Wherever major concentrations of drawings coincide with high escarpments, many flat rocks from the bottom to the top are polished smooth and all patina is worn off from constant use as seats or perches. It is not difficult to envision these as choice seats from which to view a ceremony taking place on the canyon floor.

At two Late Period sites in Sheep Canyon (see figures on next page) there are drawings of men wearing sheep horns. One carries ceremonial objects (sheep horn, snakes?). The hunting tribes of North America have often worn headdresses with the horns of deer and buffalo during ceremonial dances. At two other sites (Iny-40 and Iny-43), sheep horns appear to be mounted on sticks which were probably sunk into the ground at the ceremonial site.

An unusual pecked panel at Iny-43, features a human figure drawn in a very sophisiticated manner. He is bearing a fringed object on his back and is reaching for a weighted atlatl. Other items in the integrated composition include an unidentified object similar to the one portrayed in the figure at the top of page 40 and a spiral of dots connecting the figure with what appears to be a sheep head mounted on a stick. The rest of the drawing has broken away at some time after the picture was made (see figure bottom page 40).

The odd two-headed sheep that often occur during the Late Period had completely puzzled us. A friend who had been raised on a farm has suggested it may symbolize a

Figures With Sheep Horn Headdresses From Sheep Canyon (Late Period).

sheep birth. One head is always drawn much smaller than the other and might represent the invariable head-first appearance of many animals at birth. This would tie in with the hope for an increase in the numbers of sheep. The pictures of sheep inside sheep would also fit this theory.

The evidence of the rock pictures indicates that the sheep cult with its attendant ceremonies was the most elaborate form of religion known to the early inhabitants of the region. When the first studies were made of the customs of the Indians in the area, the remnant population had no faintest memory of the rock drawing or sheep hunting ritual. Their main ceremonies were the annual round dance, vaguely slanted toward the hope for all good things, and the individual routines of the shaman.

To recapitulate, economically important game species were treated ceremonially when killed by many North American tribes. This was to placate the spirit of the slain creature

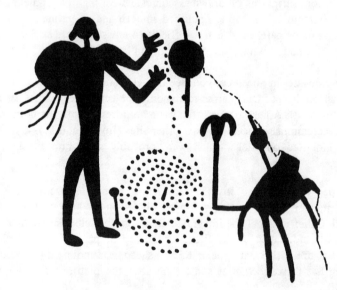

Unusual Ceremonial Figure With Atlatl. There is one element here that looks like a sheep skull mounted on a stick. Note unidentified ceremonial object at man's feet (same as middle figure above) (Iny-43).

so that it would return to the hunter in a new body, ready to be taken again. The evidence of the rock drawings in the Coso Range indicates the observance of such rites for the sheep. In addition, the constant picturing on stone of the wary animal must have been considered helpful in bringing hunter success. It is also possible that the sheep came to be regarded as a benign supernatural deity capable of aiding and protecting the individual and the group. Only on the basis of such assumptions can one understand such a vast concentration of sheep drawings.

It is not known what ended the ritual hunting of sheep in the area. By the time the first whites arrived in the Coso region in the 1860's no communal hunts were being undertaken, and in fact, the sparse Indian population at the start of the historic period was inadequate for such hunts. Linguistic studies have traced the Numic-speaking Shoshoneans that occupied huge areas of the western United States at the beginning of the historic period, to a starting point in southeastern California and southern Nevada. These migrations, which depopulated southeastern California and settled regions as far north as Wyoming and east into Texas, began 1000 or more years ago according to Lamb (1958), or as recently as A.D. 1200 (Heizer and Baumhoff, 1962).

There are archaeological clues from southern Nevada to back up the linguistic evidence of the migrations. There were extensive Anasazi settlements along the Muddy and lower Virgin Rivers in the form of pit houses and surface houses. The influence of these Pueblo people extended over a wide area, and evidence of their hunting and trading parties has been found as far west as Death Valley on the California border. By about A.D. 1150, these villages had been abandoned, and according to Shutler (1961), it was the increasing pressure of the Shoshonean Southern Paiute that forced the eastward withdrawal of the Anasazi. The Southern Paiute were in complete control of the region in historic times.

The Coso people were undoubtedly an important segment of the Shoshonean migrations. What made them leave? Geist (1967) has studied the bighorn band habits in the Northwest and his conclusions may shed some light on the disappearance of the Coso bighorn population and the end of the hunting cult. The mountain sheep will stay on their ancient home ranges, generation after generation, without the slightest variation *unless* killed off or hunted excessively by man. The evidence of the rock pictures indicates that the harassment and killing by the Coso hunters became so excessive that the bands were destroyed and the remnants driven from the area. According to Geist, the reasons for the inflexible feeding patterns of the bighorn are to be found in the social organization of the bands. The lambs from birth follow the ewe bands acquiring knowledge of the traditional feeding grounds for winter and summer, migration routes between these grounds, location of salt licks, and watering areas. There is no such thing as foraging by individuals away from the band. Once driven off their home range, the sheep will not reinhabit the area and adapt to new territory very slowly as new patterns are learned.

In an attempt to answer some of the puzzling questions involving the disappearance of the Coso bighorn and the Shoshonean migrations, we suggest the following theory.

In the Early Period, the Coso hunters armed with the relatively inefficient atlatl, used rock pictures as an important psychological or hunting-magic aid. The evidence of early

Spanish explorers shows that the numbers of bighorn in the Great Basin and in the Southwest were enormous and well able to withstand such hunting pressure as the Coso atlatl hunters could bring to bear. With the introduction of the bow, a great step forward was taken in the art of killing game. With the bow as prime weapon and the development of large communal hunts, the kill rate must have gone up sharply. Excavations at Danger Cave, Utah (Jennings, 1957) indicate the effectiveness of the bow over the atlatl. Level IV (mainly bow and arrow) shows a 280% increase in ungulate bones over Level V (mainly atlatl). The use of dogs, beaters, and dummy hunters along the cliffs, and especially ambushing on the migration routes through canyons, helped make a large harvest of sheep possible. It has been suggested that bands of sheep might have been driven over cliffs in certain areas—a deadly method of mass extermination successfully used against buffalo in many parts of the West. The dummy hunters would have been useful for such a hunting technique.

A point, of maximum killing we believe, was reached in the Late Period and brought on the development of a sheep cult, a period when the rock pictures suggest the animal was revered as an object of worship and veneration. It is probable that with the improved hunting techniques, hunting magic was no longer the main motivation for the pictures. Somewhere along the line however, the point of overkill and insupportable harassment of the bighorn was reached, causing them to abandon the area. This in turn could have brought on an intensification of sheep ritual to bring the sheep back. But, as Geist points out, they don't come back. The good times created by the bow and an ample and supposedly inexhaustible food supply abruptly ended. In a small way it was the story of the buffalo and the rifle.

With the sheep gone, the cult died out and with it, the long tradition of making rock pictures. It is possible that the destruction of the Coso bighorn bands coincided with the beginning of the Shoshonean migrations. Another factor that doubtless helped to trigger the Shoshonean migrations was the gradual drying out of the country and the disappearance of the great Pleistocene lakes (see the figure on page 5). When the first whites arrived in the 1860's, only the remnant of Owens Lake still existed.

Though the tradition of making rock designs died out in the Coso area, we know that in many places where the Shoshonean migrants wandered, they took their sheep beliefs with them. Sheep drawings are abundant in the Four Corners region, particularly in southeastern Utah. At one site in northern Arizona, there are patterned-body anthropomorphs so similar to some in the Coso Range that their common origin seems unmistakable (see figure on page 123).

Though this chapter has been mainly concerned with the interpretation of the rock drawings in relation to hunting magic, some of them, particularly the early abstract patterns and the Late Period shield-like designs might relate to other matters. In parts of the western states much of the rock art was made in connection with puberty rites, fertility, weather control, and clan identification. There is no ethnographic evidence for the purpose of the drawings in the Coso Range and the only clues lie in the subject matter itself. This subject matter bears witness to an immense preoccupation with bighorn sheep and the hunting of bighorn sheep.

7. DATING THE ROCK DRAWINGS

It is not possible to tell exactly how old a particular rock engraving in the Coso region might be. In certain areas in North America, there is ethnological information from Indians who actually made rock pictures when they were young, during puberty ceremonies. Such instances are rare—in most cases we can only know in a general way the age of the drawings.

Relative dating can be arrived at in a number of ways: through differential patination and erosion, superimposition, and subject matter.

Approximate dating is possible by relating subject matter to archaeological deposits, especially those containing perishable material that can be dated by the radiocarbon method.

In the following section, each method will be discussed in detail.

PATINA, EROSION, AND LICHEN OVERGROWTH

Certain rocks in the western states, particularly basaltic lava and sandstone, undergo a process of weathering that turns the surface much darker than the interior or unaltered stone. This surface alteration varies from medium brown to intense blue-black in its final phase, and is known as patina. Where the patinated surface has been exposed to the scouring action of dust and fine sand, the blackened rock acquires a glossy varnished effect and the term "desert varnish" is often used to describe such patina on rocks.

There are various theories to account for desert varnish. Flamand (1921) investigated the formation of patina in the desert regions of North Africa, a country of dry climate and occasional rain storms, not unlike our own western deserts. He attributes the surface darkening to the following process. Rainwater soaks into the rock surface and then is brought back to the surface through capillary action, depositing on the surface various chemicals in the rock such as carbonates, silicates and iron oxides. The process requires neither too much nor too little moisture. In addition to the surface darkening by deposition of soluble chemicals, there seems to be darkening caused by action of strong sunlight. Flamand also noted that the thickness of the layer affected by patination continued to increase slowly with time.

A. R. Willcox (1963) has studied the rock-pecked drawings of South Africa. These are on igneous rocks (dolorite, diabase, hornfels) located in the central highlands, a high desert country of hot summers, cold winters and rainfall (with frequent summer thunderstorms), remarkably like that of the Petroglyph–Renegade Canyon region. He describes the same process for the formation of patina first noted by Flamand, but adds some additional details. The leaching out of the minerals (chiefly iron and manganese) increases the porosity of the zone immediately below the patina; this weathered zone changes color to a brown buff and is much softer than the unaltered rock below. The mineral salts deposited on the surface tend to fill in small surface irregularities, facilitating the polishing action of wind and sand. The rock surface remains constant while being abraded away because fresh minerals in solution are constantly being brought to the surface to replace the loss. Thus both patina and weathering zone beneath remain roughly the same thickness though continuing to retreat from the position of the original surface.

Another theory was described by Laudermilk (1931), in which he suggests that desert varnish is caused by the decomposition of a certain lichen and its spores which contain a high content of iron and manganese salts. Subsequently the salts are oxidized through exposure to intense sunlight.

According to Hunt (1954), the desert varnish in the Colorado Plateau was formed through the action of ample rainfall and sunlight, and the darkest deposits must have been formed during the Great Pluvial accompanying the last phase of the Wisconsin Glaciation, perhaps 10,000 to 15,000 years ago. Donald Martin of Santa Rosa does not agree with Hunt on this. He has collected heavily patinated rocks from the China Lake region and exposed them to the weather in Santa Rosa where the summers are warm and dry and the winters cool and wet with rainfall over 30 inches. Within two years, all desert varnish had vanished.

The clue afforded by Martin's experiment, a study of the scanty literature on the subject, and much field work throughout the west by the senior author has led to the following conclusions. The evidence is plain that wherever patina or desert varnish appears, the two basic agents are heat and moisture. The principal regions where patina forms are arid with frequent summer thundershowers. Frequently such showers furnish most of the annual rainfall. These thundershowers sometimes drop great amounts of water very quickly in a spotty and erratic manner and in the west are called cloudbursts. One small area can be deluged during such a storm while country a mile away remains dry.

It seems evident that *optimum formation of patina occurs only in areas where high summer temperatures and thundershowers occur together.* Thus it is not just that moisture and heat both play a part in patina formation, but that this heat and moisture must occur *at the same time.* The sequence would be that first the superheated rock is soaked by rain from a thundershower, following which the sun comes out and reheats the rock. The moisture that has penetrated the rock returns to the surface through capillary action carrying minute quantities of minerals in solution. These minerals are oxidized by air action and when combined with intense heat, form patina. The summer heat and cold winter rains at Santa Rosa destroyed the patina. If this theory is correct, desert varnish could not have formed during a cool, wet pluvial. This in turn would indicate that the Mojave Desert patina began to form sometime *after* the end of the Great Pluvial (9,000 to 4,000 years ago), as the country was becoming hotter and dryer or *after* the Little Pluvial (4,000 to 3,000 years ago).

All writers agree that desert varnish is formed very slowly, and it is this feature that makes relative dating of rock engravings cut into the patina possible. Presumably then, as soon as the rock drawing is shallowly pecked or abraded through the desert varnish to the brownish, weathered zone, or deeply pecked to the unaltered rock beneath, a repatination of the cut surface commences. Eventually, over a long period of time, the lines of the engraving again become patinated to the same color as the surrounding rock and the design can then only be seen by an oblique light that shadows the engraved lines.

Thus if on a single rock surface, you find drawings that are strong in contrast, others that have lost all contrast, and still others that seem half-way between these two extremes, you have a relative chronology. At China Lake we often have seen two of these phases and rarely all three on a single panel.

An Example of Complete Repatination. The design is only visible because the shiny surface of the unpecked rock reflects the light.

Relative patination can give us, in a general way, a relative chronology, but there are so many variables that too much reliance cannot be placed on this method of dating without careful correlation with other factors such as style, subject matter, and erosion. Our investigations in the Coso region have discovered these variable factors affecting patination: Not all of the basalts in the area are of the same type. Some are weathering through sand-blasting faster than the patina can reform, while other surfaces are being eroded at a rate slow enough to allow patina to keep forming. Upper surfaces of rocks receive more heat than vertical surfaces and are usually more heavily patinated. Surfaces facing up or down canyon tend to wind-scour heavily and inhibit formation of patina. Rock faces close to the sandy bottom of the canyons are more subject to wind erosion. In some sections where the action of blown sand has slowed desert varnish deposition, water seeps after thundershowers have flowed over certain parts of the rock, leaving dark patinated streaks. In these cases, the extra moisture has tipped the scale in favor of the patina. In one instance, such a seep has turned one section of a rock design dark, while the part not affected by the seep is still quite light.

A Panel in R-25 Showing Deeper Patina Where Water Has Seeped Over the Rock Surface.

We have found very few completely patinated rock drawings in the Coso Range, not more than a dozen. Because of the variable factors affecting rate of desert varnish formation, these cannot be definitely called the oldest engravings in the region.

There is a problem that we encountered in the Coso investigations that has yet to be solved. At some sites much of the rock has been weathered to a brownish buff color, the surface is dull and there is little patina. Nearby masses of rock may be blue-black and shiny. Experiments with a cutting tool showed that the weathered surface of pale rock was easily cut, while the black rock was cut with difficulty. Freshly broken surfaces of the two types look remarkably similar. If the two rock are actually *different*, it must mean that one is susceptible to surface decay and the other is resistant.

There are many drawings in Renegade Canyon where surfaces covered with drawings of the Early and Transitional Period are severely eroded. The heaviest erosion occurs where the panel faces up or down canyon where it is subject to strong wind and sand blasting. It is possible that the pecking itself (often covering as much as half of the panel) makes the surface more susceptible to erosion by roughening it. A rough surface gives the flying grains of sand something to bite into.

This roughening of the surface creates another interesting phenomenon. Often the incised lines of a design will be covered with lichen growth where the surrounding smooth surface will have little or no lichen. The wind-borne lichen spores can find easier lodgement where the design has cut into the rock.

The phenomenon of rocks being cracked and split by sudden changes in temperature is well known, and during the last century, rock engravings were quarried for a Vienna museum by lighting a fire against the face of the rock and throwing water on the hot rock, causing it to shatter. Nature is constantly performing this feat in the Coso Range. The cold summer thundershowers falling on super-heated rocks are largely responsible for the ceaseless fracturing of the basalt blocks. These freshly broken rocks offer ideal rough surfaces for lichen spores to take hold.

There is an immense amount of lichen growth at many of the Coso Range sites, especially on the north-facing surfaces, and it often is growing *over* the prehistoric designs. A number of species are represented, making a brilliant display of red, green, yellow and orange against the dark rocks. When the growth rates of these lichens have been established, they may give dates for some of the Late Period rock drawings.

Ronald Beschel, a Canadian investigator, has made studies on the growth rate of Arctic lichens (Beschel, 1961). The growth rate varies considerably depending on the species, type of rock, and climate, but all types grow slowly and some of the crust-lichens grow but a fraction of a millimeter per year.

For such growth determinations, it is necessary to know when the rock was first exposed to air-borne lichen spores. This is possible with some volcanic rocks, rocks emerging from drained lakes, gravestones, and the like.

Lichen Growing Over Drawings at (R-23).

47

A Deeply Pecked Sheep From a Streambed Level Location. The water had completely destroyed the patina, but the depth of the pecking enabled the drawing to stand out when obliquely lighted.

Lichen growth studies have great possibilities in solving dating problems on the more recent rock engravings (some lichen species are known to reach an age of around 700 years). Dr. Beschel has estimated the age of a lichen-encrusted Eskimo site as at least 500 years old (Taylor, 1963), and Gerhard Folmann, using Beschel's methods, has given an average age of 430 years to the great stone figures on Easter Island (Folmann, 1961).

The sand-bearing streams of the pluvial periods have carved deeply into the basalt in the gorge sections of Petroglyph and Renegade Canyons, and intermittant flood water down to the present time has kept desert varnish from forming on the canyon floor. In the upper end of Renegade (section 25), there are Early Period drawings deeply cut into the pale gray water-scoured basalt at streambed level. There is no contrast whatsoever between design and surrounding rock, but the deep cutting of the design allows it to stand out when sunlight strikes the rock surface obliquely.

SEQUENCE OF HUNTING WEAPONS

The evidence is conclusive that man entered the New World as a hunter at least 12,000 years ago. Early sites in the Southwest and in the high plains have yielded the bones of extinct mammals such as the mammoth, ground sloth, giant bison, and horse in association with large, finely flaked and fluted points of the Clovis type. It is probable that these points were mounted on stout thrusting and throwing spears. There is no evidence that these earliest hunters possessed the spear-thrower or atlatl.

48

In this discussion, we will use the Uto-Aztecan (Nahuatl) word, atlatl. This curious weapon has been used by prehistoric man for a very long time. Spear-throwers of bone and ivory have been found in Magdalenian deposits in France and Switzerland that have been dated at between 10,000 and 15,000 years old. The atlatl has many variations, but the principal remains the same. In the Great Basin, it was a flat stick usually from 18 to 24 inches long, equipped with a hand grip at one end, often with leather finger loops or notches for the first and second fingers. At the other end, there was a projecting or recessed hook to engage with a depression in the butt of the spear or dart. The atlatl was held alongside the shoulder (see figure on page 50), and in action, provided an extra joint to the human arm as it lifted the spear high and forward on the thrust. Considerable accuracy and great force were possible at short ranges.

Type 1 (without finger-grips), 75% of total.

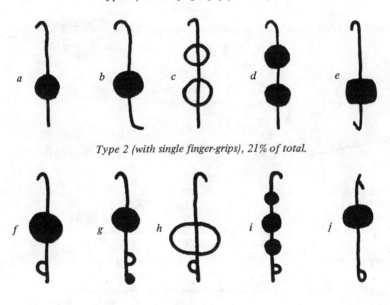

Type 2 (with single finger-grips), 21% of total.

Type 3 (with double finger-grips), 4% of total.

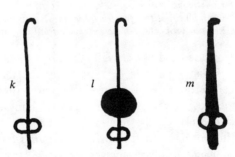

The Three Basic Types of Atlatls Found in the Coso Range. Type 1 is the oldest and most numerous variety. The final development, Type 3, is rare; there is only one example of the m variety. a, d, e, and i, (R-25); b, c, g, h, and m, (R-35); f, (P-4); j, (Iny-26); and k and l, (P-9).

At an early period, the use of this weapon became wide-spread in the Old World. It became (and still is) the chief hunting weapon of the Australian aborigines. It was taken into the New World, possibly by Australoid migration, and eventually reached the tip of South America. Just how ancient this introduction might be in the Great Basin region is impossible to say, but atlatl dart fragments from the Leonard Rock Shelter in Nevada give a radiocarbon date of 7038 ± 350 years ago. As the atlatl was invariably made of wood, fragments of the weapon can only have survived in dry caves. Many pieces of atlatls and darts have been found buried under rocks and sand in such caves and even a few complete specimens have been recovered (see figures on page 53). Grosscup (1960) has analyzed the artifact material recovered from Lovelock Cave, Nevada, a site continuously occupied for about 3000 years (roughly from 2000 B.C. until A.D. 1000). According to Grosscup, atlatl fragments occurred from the earliest period until about 1 B.C. The bow first appeared about 500 B.C. and completely supplanted the atlatl by 1 B.C.

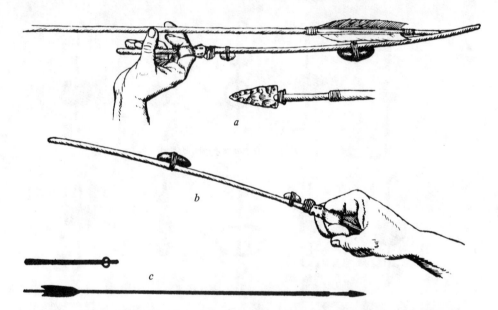

The Atlatl in Action. These drawings were made using an exact model of a Basketmaker atlatl from a burial cave in northeastern Arizona (Guernsey, 1931). a. Position at beginning of cast with dart gripped lightly between thumb and first two fingers. Insert shows attachment of point to foreshaft. b. Position at end of cast. c. Relative proportion of Basketmaker atlatl to dart.

The bow introduced from Asia did not arrive in the Great Basin and the Southwest until relatively recent times. Its appearance in the Four Corners region (Anasazi) was not until about A.D. 200 and coincidental with the introduction of unfired pottery. The Lovelock dates indicate that the bow, far superior as a general hunting weapon, very slowly replaced the atlatl that had been in use thousands of years. There are, of course, certain advantages the spear-thrower has over the bow: it can hurl a far heavier projectile and it can be used with one hand; its disadvantages are its relative slowness of flight, less penetrating power, and less accuracy at longer range.

Farmer (1955) describes some specific sites in the Southwest where there are approximate dates for the introduction of the bow:

After the atlatl or spear-thrower went out of use, the bow came to be the major weapon. This change has not yet been fully documented but in some areas some dates can be suggested. Some arrow foreshafts were found in Canyon del Muerte in a Basketmaker II site (roughly A.D. 200 to 400) (Morris, 1939), and at Obelisk Cave the finds suggest that the bow and arrow had displaced the atlatl before 700 A.D. (Morris, 1936). Material at Tularosa Cave in west central New Mexico shows that the Mogollon people made increasing use of the bow after 700 A.D. (Martin and others, 1952). Evidence at Ventana Cave in southern Arizona shows the use of the bow perhaps as early as 1 A.D. In the Trans-Pecos area of west Texas the atlatl-bow sequence had been noted with a possible date for the introduction of the bow at about 900 A.D. (Kelley, 1950).

These dates, together with the Lovelock Cave dating, make it possible to draw the simple map below, tracing by relative chronology the possible movement of the bow through the

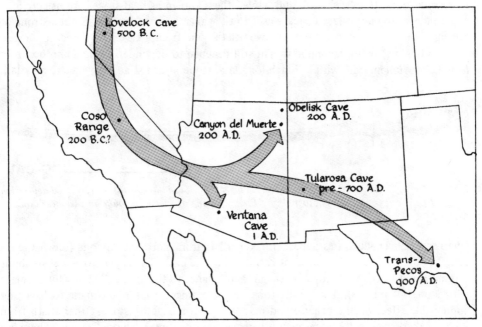

Earliest Occurrences of the Bow in the Great Basin and the Southwest (Grosscup, 1960; Morris, 1936, 1939; Martin and others, 1952; Kelley, 1950) With a Suggested Progression of Introduction.

Great Basin and into the Southwest. The Obelisk Cave date indicates that in the Four Corners region it took about 500 years for the bow to completely supplant the atlatl, a conclusion that is remarkably like that reached by Grosscup for the Lovelock Cave material.

There is historical evidence that the atlatl continued in use well into the historical period in certain regions of North America. In 1542, De Soto's men at the mouth of the Mississippi discovered that the atlatl used by the Indians was an efficient and dangerous weapon. Johann Jacob Baegert, a Jesuit missionary at the San Luis Gonzaga Mission in Baja California, noted that the local Indians had the bow-and-arrow but still used the spear-thrower as late as the mid 1700's. The weapon continued in use among the Eskimo until modern times, and on Lake Patzcuaro in Michoacan, Mexico, the Tarascan Indians still employ the atlatl to throw a three-pronged spear in duck hunting.

There are only three areas in North America where the atlatl is pictured in rock art. The first is in western Texas, particularly along the lower Pecos River where Jackson (1938); and Kirkland and Newcomb (1967) describe a number of atlatl sites. The second is in the San Juan River drainage of southeastern Utah where there are two recorded instances (the Texas and Utah drawings do not show weights attached to weapon), and the third region is in the desert ranges of southeastern California and southern Nevada, with a major concentration in the Coso Range. Here they are associated with the earliest-appearing drawings and occur in great numbers. At the major sites, there are many representations of the weapon, usually highly stylized with a stone weight (greatly exaggerated in size) attached to the atlatl. These weights have been found in many places in the United States, and for a long time their use was unknown. Some, particularly from near the Columbia River, are round to oval-shaped, and while others known as boat-stones are usually long and slender with one surface concave as if to fit against a curved surface. Emory Strong of Portland has sent us photographs of two atlatls—one from a cave near Condon, Oregon (pictured below), with decorated weight still fastened to the underside, and another from near Lake Winnemucca, with a 7-inch-long boat-stone attached at both ends to an atlatl.

10 cm

Profile View of Small Atlatl With Sheep Horn Finger-grips. Stone weight fits into recessed depression in wood (wrapping restored). Photograph by Emory Strong of specimen found in cave near Condon, Oregon.

Guernsey (1931) illustrates a Basketmaker atlatl from northern Arizona (see figure on page 50) that had several small stones attached to the back. The larger stone weighs about 2 ounces and would certainly give weight and balance to the light oak atlatl (total weight with stones—4 ounces). The small stone near the finger grips is too light to have any appreciable effect on the balance and may be a charm or fetish stone. Other atlatls from Basketmaker caves in the same region have as many as three such small stones. There is a possibility they served a double purpose as balance weights and charmstones. Often the Coso atlatl drawings show 2 or 3 stones attached to the weapon.

Complete atlatl spears or darts have been recovered from cave caches and burials in northeastern Arizona. The mainshafts averaged 54 inches long and were feathered in the same manner as an arrow. The hardwood foreshafts, about 6 inches long, were inserted into the bored end of the mainshaft and secured with sinew wrapping. Nearly all of the darts and arrows of the Great Basin and Southwest were made in this two-part manner. The foreshaft and projectile point were designed to do the killing with the mainshaft carrying the warhead to its mark. Bags of tipped foreshafts have been found—obviously carried as spares during the hunt.

Curiosity about the efficiency of the atlatl prompted us to make an exact facsimile of the Basketmaker weapon described above, and of the typical hunting dart. As material for the mainshaft of the dart, we used Giant Rye grass (*Elymus condensatus*), which grows to a height of over 14 feet in the Santa Barbara region and makes a strong, very light shaft. A second material slightly heavier but stonger than the Giant Rye is Tree Tobacco (*Nicotiana glauca*). This lacks the internodes of the Giant Rye and is less subject to breakage.

We found that longer distances were achieved when the 2-ounce stone weight was removed. A 2 1/4-ounce dart was thrown ten times for an average cast of 195 feet and one cast measured 240 feet. At close ranges (from 50 to 75 feet) the weapon proved astonishingly accurate. These are approximately the ranges used by the ancient sheep hunters of the Coso Range as demonstrated by distances from the hunting blinds to the canyon floor below where the game would be driven. The stone weight seemed to give the close shots more thrust and penetration, but the conclusion is inescapable that the main function of the stones must have been as charmstones to bring added magic to bear on the problem of hunter success.

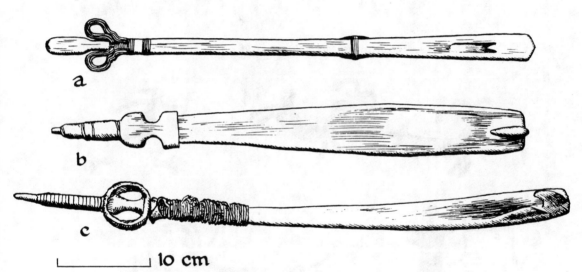

a

b

c

└──────────┘ **10 cm**

Typical Atlatl Designs. A. Basketmaker II (A.D. 200–400). Redrawn from Kidder and Guernsey (1919); b. Great Basin raised-spur atlatl (upper surface) Cressman (1942); c. Complete raised spur atlatl from Lake Winnemucca, Nevada, region cave. Note bone tip on handle for reflaking damaged points and raised ridge near spur to support dart. Curved shape of atlatl is typical. From original specimen at the Nevada State Historical Society.

Malcolm Hill (1947) made exhaustive tests with various types and weights of atlatls and darts and arrived at much the same conclusions. He found that light darts (3/4 ounce to 1-1/4 ounce) and unweighted atlatl were best for long distance.

The use of the spear thrower has persisted among the Australian aborigines, and the following information from McCarthy (1957) shows what a formidable weapon it is in the hands of people trained to its use from childhood.

The Australian spear thrower, or wommara, varies from 20 inches to 45 inches in length, and in Northern Australia is either of the flat lath type or the rounded stick type (often

Figures holding weighted atlatls. a, b, (P-9), c, (P-8), d, e, (R-25).

Figures hunting with bow and arrow f, (R-35), h, (S-16), i, j, (P-9). Note the ultimate stylization of archer in i.

with a knob end). In central and southern Australia, the spear thrower is leaf- or spindle-shaped. There are no finger grips. The spears are longer and heavier than those in the New World—8 to 10 feet..

With the hand-thrown spear, the aborigines can cast up to 70 feet. With the wommara, there are recorded casts up to 390 feet. The weapon is extremely accurate on stationary targets to 180 feet and on moving targets to 75 feet.

The number of atlatl drawings tallied are as follows: Renegade, 261; Petroglyph, 21; Sheep, 28. These figures would indicate that Renegade was exploited for hunting at an earlier period than the other canyons. The figures for these same canyons for the bowmen are as follows: Renegade, 61; Petroglyph, 118; Sheep, 40. These figures on the bowmen show a marked upswing of the later hunting symbols in Petroglyph and Sheep Canyons which came into heavy use for hunting and attendant ceremonies in the Transitional and Late Periods.

Just how or when the bow first arrived in the Coso region is unknown, but it is our guess that it was sometime after its appearance in the Lovelock Cave area or sometime between 500 B.C. and 1 B.C. It might have been introduced by migratory newcomers moving down the eastern slope of the Sierra Nevada, or through tribe-to-tribe contact. In any case, it seems likely that the light-weight Shoshonean arrow point appeared at the same time as the bow.

During the Transitional Period, chiefly characterized by the shift from the atlatl to the bow, a few drawings (six instances) were made of men holding the atlatl, but this revolutionary departure from the simple depiction of the weapon alone must have come near the end of the atlatl era, or we would find more examples of it. During the Late Period, the atlatl was no longer shown and it can be presumed that the early weapon had been entirely superseded by the bow.

At one of the Little Lake sites (Iny-26), there is a concentration of over 30 atlatls. Five of these appear relatively late, contrary to the overwhelming evidence of the transition of weapons in the region. There is ethnographic evidence that recent Indians often copied ancient designs "just for fun" with no slightest knowledge of the meaning of such designs (Gifford, 1936, p. 290 and Haury, 1945, p. 70). In addition, two of these recent appearing atlatls depict weights so foreign to the usual type that they can be written off as the creations of people who did not know the meaning or function of these rock designs (see Figure Iny-26 in Surrounding Sites Section on page 97). It is also possible that the atlatl was retained as an object of ritual importance or as a status symbol long after it ceased to be a prime weapon for hunting, just as Western man continues to wear the military sword for full dress parades and ceremonial occasions.

In the Coso Range we have the most graphic record of the disappearance of the atlatl and the introduction of the bow. The relative dating is unquestioned, and design elements that can be associated with the weapons by differential patination or erosion can be assigned the same relative age. It is hoped that the numerous caves discovered during the Coso rock drawing survey may produce perishable weapon material that will give us dates for the beginnings of bow hunting, and thus for the earliest bow drawings.

Two Occupation Caves Near (R-25).

SUPERIMPOSITION

The superimposition of one drawing on top of another is often a good guide to relative age, but in the Coso region it is not of much help. Usually the superimpositions appear to be of the same period as the under-designs with the possibility of ritual obliteration or because certain rocks were thought to have more "power" than unused rocks nearby. In cases where differences in patina showed that the superimposed drawing was later, the style and subject matter of both levels is usually so similar that the only conclusion that can be drawn is that basic art forms remained constant for long periods of time.

Certain combinations occur with enough frequency to form a pattern. Abstract designs are almost invariably *under* naturalistic drawings. Sheep with horns to the front are *always* over sheep with horns in profile. The most frequent examples of superimposition are large sheep over elaborate patterned-body anthropomorphs and here again both seem of about the same, if not identical, age.

ASSOCIATION WITH ARCHAEOLOGICAL MATERIALS

At the Stahl Cave just above Little Lake, there are crude drawings of sheep and bowmen pecked on the inside of the cave. Excavation of the cave (Harrington, 1957) has revealed that the cave had been used by Pinto Basin people at least 3,000 years ago, and that more than 1,000 years ago, Early and Late Basketmaker people had lived there. Finally the cave was used by Shoshonean people who were the first who had used the cave to have the bow.

Our own feelings about the Stahl cave dwellers are based on our work in Petroglyph and Renegade Canyons where the style and subject matter reflect an orderly change by the same people; Harrington's three or four groups could easily have been the same group passing through slight cultural changes.

Projectile points are found in abundance near all the major sites, usually on the mesas directly above the gorges. These follow the Stahl site pattern. There are heavy, crudely flaked atlatl points of the Pinto Basin type, and small, delicately flaked Shoshonean arrow points. A clearer picture can be obtained on cultural association and approximate dating when more archaeological work is done in the Coso Range, particularly when some of the caves adjacent to rock drawing sites are excavated.

POSSIBLE DATING OF COSO RANGE ROCK DRAWINGS

The chart on page 58 gives our tentative estimate on the dating of the Coso drawings. While admittedly speculative, it is based on the evidence presented in this book. The two most important age factors are the weapon transition from atlatl to bow and variable patination. There is a strong possibility that the existing patina began forming after the Little Pluvial of 3000 to 4000 years ago when warm summers and thundershowers allowed the desert varnish to build up. This would mean that no drawings could be much older than 3000 years.

For the Coso Transitional Period marking the appearance of the bow and the disappearance of the atlatl, we are giving a starting date of 200 B.C. and a terminal date of A.D. 300. This is roughly between Grosscup's dating for the Lovelock Cave bow introduction and the first appearance of the bow in northeastern Arizona. In both these areas, the Transitional Period lasted about 500 years.

An Example of Superimposition Where Earlier Drawings Are Noticeably Deeper in Patination Than Big Sheep (P-9).

It is difficult to assign a terminal date to the Late Period, but there are a number of clues. Sometime around 1000 years ago (Lamb 1958) the three branches of the Numic Shoshonean people began to migrate from southeastern California and southern Nevada to the east and northeast. In the chapter on Interpretation, we have stated our belief that a vital factor in starting the Coso area migrations might have been the disappearance of the sheep. Further, it is probable that the introduction of the bow led to the climactic harassment of the bighorn that drove the remnants of the once great bands from the region, and that this in turn ended the long tradition of rock art making. Based on this reasoning, we have arbitrarily placed the end of the Late Period around A.D. 1000. Later dating of weapon fragments from the excavations of the Coso caves may, of course, throw our postulated age for the Coso Range drawings off by many hundreds of years.

The painted sites are certainly late, but how late is difficult to say. They are mainly on exposed surfaces subject to erosion and cannot be too old. We have given them a rough dating of post A.D. 1700. The pit-and-groove petroglyphs fall in the Early Period, though some show superficial repecking done during the Late Period or possibly by Indians of historic times to increase the contrast.

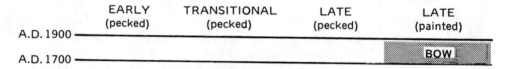

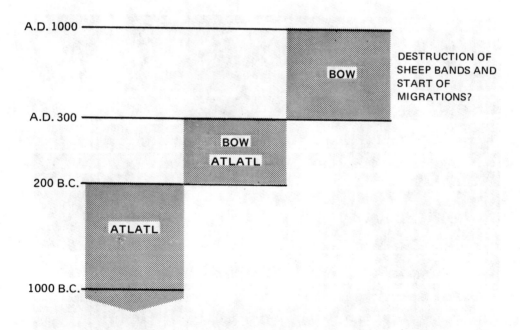

A Possible Dating With the Relationship Between Coso Rock Art Styles and the Transition of Weapons.

8. THE MAJOR SITES

The site designations in parentheses—(P-4), etc.—will enable the reader to quickly locate the sites on the map below. For example, (P-4) locates that part of Petroglyph Canyon that runs through Section 4. All the major sites can be located on the U.S.G.S. topographical map for Coso Peak.

PETROGLYPH CANYON

The canyon is approached from the northeast on a 4-mile jeep track that meets the Coso Hot Springs-Junction Ranch road about 7 miles west of Etcheron Valley. The jeep road is partly in a sandy wash and partly over boulder-strewn mesa.

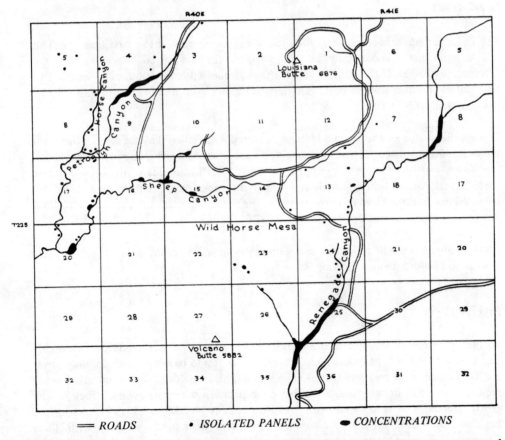

=== ROADS   • ISOLATED PANELS   ▬ CONCENTRATIONS

This map Is Part of the USGS Topographical Map "COSO PEAK." Numbered sections measure 1 square mile. To relate the map to the site descriptions: (P-4) is that part of Petroglyph Canyon in Section 4, etc.

Petroglyph Canyon Looking North Toward the Main Concentration at (P-9).

Iny-7 (P-4)

The first drawings are found where the shallow canyon narrows into a basaltic gorge. This is a formula that is almost universal in this region: the carvings are concentrated at the entrances to gorges. If the gorge is short, the drawings will continue the full length. In a long gorge (anything over a mile), the designs usually do not continue for more than a few hundred yards.

The southeast side of the canyon is largely covered with lichen that has often grown over the engravings. This upper part of Petroglyph contains the largest group of shield designs. The finest and best-preserved examples are on the northwest side of the canyon where there is little or no lichen growth and where the rocks have a darker patination. We recorded one hunting blind of piled stones on the northwest side of the canyon and about 30 feet from the bottom. Total drawings—1047.

(P-4) is about one-half mile long and terminates at a low point on both sides of the canyon just before it enters Section 9.

Iny-7A (P-9)

At the upper end of (P-9) there is a high basaltic cliff on the northwest side. It is highly fractured into many large blocks and is covered from top to base with rock drawings, over 2,000 of them in an area less than 400 feet long. This is the densest concentration in the region. There is a draw opposite the big concentration where every small rock on the gently sloping rise is covered with pictures, mainly of sheep. This cliff marks the beginning of a deep gorge that continues without a break to the junction with Horse Canyon 1 1/2 miles below. The engravings in (P-9) are mainly on the northwest side. The drawings get fewer and fewer as you continue down the gorge and after about 1/3 of a mile, they disappear entirely.

This section contains the finest of the Late Period stylized sheep and also some of the best patterned-body anthropomorphs. Three of the rare drawings of men holding atlatls are in (P-9). Total drawings—3779.

Iny-7B (P-8)

As the canyon enters Section 8, there is a short distance, less than 1/4 of a mile before the junction with Horse Canyon (H-8), where there are scattered drawings. They are of the Early and Transitional Periods and include several atlatls and two men holding atlatls. These are all on the north face. The canyon is very deep here with almost sheer sides rising over 300 feet. The adjoining Section 17, below the confluence with Horse Canyon, has been partially explored (the lower two-thirds where one small single drawing was found), and it is unlikely that much has been missed. Total drawings—30.

Iny-7C (P-20)

Between the northern edge of Section 20 and the confluence of Sheep Canyon, there are a few small sites, mainly of shield patterns, directly below an occupation cave about 40 feet above the stream bed and on the west side. Total drawings—44. Just below the junction with Sheep Canyon, there is an immense rock slide on the north side of the canyon where there are many large and carefully executed sheep—about 150 drawings (these are not included in the tally table as the site was discovered just before publication).

Iny-7D (P-3)

This is the northernmost site in Petroglyph Canyon. It lies about 1 mile north of the upper end of Iny-7, to the right of the road on a low promontory. The subjects are sheep, deer, and miscellaneous abstract patterns. Approximate number—25.

This Late Period Panel Shows a Weightless Atlatl (Type 3). During this period the atlatl had ceased to be the chief weapon but possibly continued to be used as a ceremonial object or status symbol (P-9).

Transitional Period. Note the ear decorations and headdresses (P-9).

Late Period (P-4).

(P-9).

Late and Transitional Periods (P-9).

Late Period Designs, Especially Medicine Bags Superimposed Over Transitional Drawings (P-9).

Late Period. Line of sheep hunt beaters? (P-9).

Some Early or Transitional Abstract Designs (P-9).

Most of the Shield-like Patterns Are Concentrated in This Section (P-4).

The Great Sheep (Late Period superimposed over Transitional and Late). The larger sheep is about 7 feet long (P-9).

Late Period Shield Patterns Over Transitional Sheep (P-4).

Late Period Sheep With Earlier Pit-and-groove Marks That Show Later Retouching (P-4).

The Ultimate Coso Stylization of the Bighorn Sheep. This very fine panel is on the northern edge of the major site in the region (P-9).

Late Period (P-9).

Late and Transitional Periods. Note the tiny archers shooting the mountainous sheep (P-9).

Transitional or Late Periods. Dogs, men, and sheep (P-4).

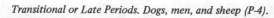

Transitional or Late Period (P-9).

Late Period (P-4).

Late Period Designs Superimposed Over Late and Transitional Motifs (P-4).

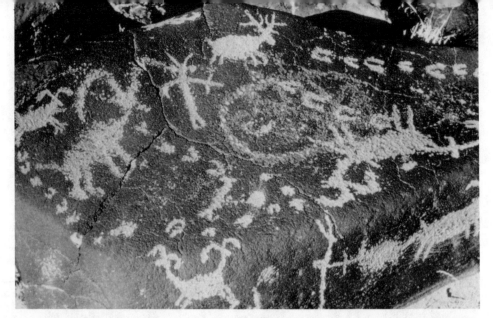

A Late Period Hunting Panel. Note two-headed sheep and sheep tracks. Drawings of deer are rare (P-9).

Late Period Sheep Superimposed Over Late or Transitional Ceremonial Figures (P-9).

Campbell Grant Photographing the Great Concentrations of Rock Drawings at (P-9).

Late Period (P-9).

Some Transitional Period Abstract Patterns (P-9).

Late Period (P-9).

69

Late Period. These lines of people could represent figures in a ceremony or beaters assembled for a sheep drive (P-9).

SHEEP CANYON

This survey has recorded a great number of new drawings in a major tributary of Petroglyph Canyon that rises on the east flank of Louisiana Butte and flows almost 10 miles to its confluence with the main canyon. It had no name and for convenient reference we have named it Sheep Canyon. Of the 2753 design elements tallied, over half were of sheep.

Iny-9 (S-10)

(S-10) is located in a short, narrow gorge on the border between Section 10 and Section 15 (west fork of Sheep Canyon). The gorge is not over 500 feet long, a typical basalt intrusion along a fault line. The petroglyphs are chiefly on the north face and near the floor of the gorge. Total drawings—167.

Iny-9A (S-15)

Below (S-10) the land opens up into the rolling tableland characteristic of Wild Horse Mesa until the west fork again becomes constricted into a gorge at its junction with the east fork. This point is on the border of Section 16 and there are many drawings here that will be described under Iny-9B. A half mile up the east fork and in the exact center of Section 15, there is a small gorge that has a large number of fine rock drawings. This gorge shows evidence of having been used as a sheep corral in historic times. On the rim of the east face, there are many piles of rocks 3 feet high. In the gorge there is one small occupation cave with bedrock milling stones and a hunting blind on the west side.

Sheep Canyon (S-16). Some fine designs are located just below the cliff rim and on isolated boulders in the rock pile in the middle of the picture.

Obsidian flakes are abundant and several Shoshonean-type side-notched points were recovered on the surrounding mesa. There were six pecked examples at this site of a rare Transitional and Late Period motif—projectile points on foreshafts. Total drawings—744.

Iny-9B (S-16)

At the confluence of the west and east fork of Sheep Canyon, another gorge begins that continues with only minor breaks for over 3 miles until it joins Petroglyph Canyon. The uppermost site is partially in Section 15, and the drawings are found on both sides of the gorge for about 500 yards. Below this area, there is a barren stretch where the gorge rapidly deepens until the rim is over 200 feet from the mesa floor. The second concentration in this section is on the northern face of the gorge just before the stream bed drops abruptly by a series of falls.

These drawings are very fresh-looking and the subject matter is of the Late Period. There are no abstract patterns and the most characteristic motifs are highly stylized sheep and medicine bags. The pictures are on isolated rocks and cliff faces and the patina is very dark. Below the falls, the basalt is of a different type, very rough and porous and unsuited for rock drawing. The next mile of gorge is quite barren. Total drawings—644.

Iny-9C (S-17)

Shortly after crossing into Section 17, the gorge opens up briefly and access from the top is possible. At the same point, there is a large jumble of smooth rocks that have broken off from an intrusion on the north face, and here there are many Late Period petroglyphs. Aside from this single concentration, there are only a few isolated figures in the half mile of canyon that crosses the southeast corner of this section. Total drawings—224.

Iny-9D (S-20)

This is the largest site in Sheep Canyon and 86% of the drawings are of sheep. It is located on scattered boulders about a mile below the last big site in Section 17 and, as usual, the concentration coincides with an intrusion of smooth basaltic rock at a point where the gorge opens up. There are many examples of archers here as well as dogs attacking sheep. The complete lack of atlatls and the fresh appearance of most of the petroglyphs marks this as a Late Period site. Total drawings—949.

Iny-9E (S-12)

This is a small site near the upper end of Sheep Canyon. There is an occupation cave here with manos and metates. Total drawings—19.

An Imaginative Rendering of a Line of Sheep That Almost Suggests Perspective (S-16).

Bowman and Sheep. The creator often drew the hunter in direct contact with his game (S-16).

Iny-9F (S-13)

This is 1/2 mile below (S-12); there are six sheep pecked on isolated boulders.

HORSE CANYON

This canyon, a minor western tributary of Petroglyph, has a watershed about 2 miles long. It is reached by a half-mile hike due west of the main concentration at Iny-7A.

Iny-10 (H-8)

A few of these drawings continue up the canyon into Section 5, but are mainly scattered along the western face of Horse Canyon on the extreme eastern edge of Section 8. There are a few atlatls and bowmen, marking this a Transitional Period area. The other motifs are predominantly sheep. Total drawings—154.

Hunter With Bighorn Sheep Headdress (S-15).

(S-15).

73

A Mixed Bag of Sheep (Rams and Ewes), Deer, and Dogs. The latter are always identified by the long tail.

The Sheep in This Canyon Are Chiefly of the Late Period and Are Better Done Than the Average Coso Sheep (S-16).

(S-15).

74

Two Carefully Executed Figures: an Archer and a Medicine Bag. The bag design has been reincised to make it larger (S-16).

(S-15).

Spirited Rendering of Dogs and Sheep (S-20).

75

Some Designs, Mainly Abstract From Near the Junction of Sheep and Petroglyph Canyons (S-17).

RENEGADE CANYON

Renegade Canyon is 4 miles east and roughly parallel to Petroglyph Canyon. It is reached by 6 miles of dirt road from Etcheron Valley.

Iny-8 (R-13)

This site is approached by jeep track from the Landmark monument at the Renegade parking area. Two miles up the right side of the shallow watercourse across Wild Horse Mesa, a basalt intrusion forms a high cliff on the northwestern side of the canyon. Drawings are scattered sparsely about halfway up the cliff on large boulders, and at the rim there is a sizable concentration. There are many chipping fragments on the mesa above this site. Total drawings—224.

Iny-8A (R-24)

One and one-half miles south from (R-13) a shallow wash bearing northwest joins the main watercourse. There are minor basaltic flows on the west side of this wash and some

Renegade Canyon Looking South (R-25).

drawings on isolated boulders. They are of poor workmanship and mainly of sheep. Total drawings—31.

Iny-8B (R-25)

This is the second largest concentration of rock pictures in the Coso area. It begins roughly at the parking area where the bronze Landmark plate is set into a large boulder. At this point, a narrow basalt gorge is entered. This gorge, for about a mile, averages about 20 feet in height and 30 feet in width. Beyond this point, in Section 35, the canyon drops dramatically off Wild Horse Mesa at a 50-foot falls. The lower canyon is deep and rough with only two recorded drawings above a *tinaja*, or rock tank, that holds some water most of the year.

The oldest appearing drawings are found in this upper part of the canyon (R-25). On the eastern rim of the gorge near the parking area, there is an immense amount of obsidian flakes, and along the basaltic rim there are many bedrock milling stones and a few deep mortar holes. There are the remains of fences across the narrow canyon, which was once used as a corral for sheep before the establishment of the Naval Weapons Center. The

Bedrock Mortars at R-25. Mortars are extremely rare in the Coso Range and occur at only three sites: (R-25), (R-8), and (Iny-13).

petroglyphs in upper Renegade are mainly of the Early and Transitional Periods. Total drawings—2310.

Iny-8C (R-35)

This is a continuation of (R-25) into Section 35. The canyon is beginning to get deeper and narrower. In this area, the bottom of the gorge is solid rock, much worn and water-sculptured by ancient torrents of the Pluvials. Where the water-borne sand has cut into the rock, there is no trace of patina and the stone surface is a light blue-gray. After a rain, this part of the canyon holds many pools of water that are heavily used by the desert animals and birds until they dry up. Rock drawings are abundant on both sides of the gorge right up to the lip of a high falls where they end abruptly. Total drawings—2004.

One-half mile due east of this area is the head of another canyon that has been named Cave Canyon. We have recorded seven occupation caves here, one containing basketry and another, pottery.

Iny-8D (R-26)

In the northeast corner of Section 35, a watercourse enters the canyon from the west. It is easy to miss as there is no obvious notch; only a small dry falls marks the confluence. When you climb this falls, the side canyon comes into view. It is a shallow drainage area with basalt outcrops for about 1/4 of a mile. The drawings are mostly on the eastern face and feature the same forms as are found in the main canyon.

Northernmost Site in Renegade Canyon. There are hundreds of designs on this 60-degree scarp (Iny-8F).

Beyond the last rock pictures, there are two rock shelters on the west face with piled-up rock walls at the entrances and milling stones. Another 1/2 mile farther and higher up the slope to the west, there is another cave in a basalt outcrop. Total drawings—125.

Iny-8E (R-23)

Following up the main drainage northwest from (R-26) into Section 23, there are a few scattered drawings and a large concentration in rock piles at the low divide to a westerly flowing watercourse. These are chiefly sheep with almost no abstract patterns. On the west face of the largest rock mass, there is a hunting blind and immediately west of that, a number of well-defined house rings, many obsidian flakes, and some milling stones. These are the only house rings that were found near the main concentrations. West of this group of pictures, we recorded only a few scattered designs. The hunting blind on the divide is strategically located where game would cross from one watershed to the other. Total drawings—407.

Iny-8F (R-8)

To the northeast of Iny-8, the basalt faulting along the canyon disappears for about 1 mile and then begins to build up again culminating at the entrance to a gorge where the cliffs are about 60 feet high (altogether there is a gap of about 1 1/2 miles between Iny-8 and Iny-8F). For 1/2 mile there are continuous rock pictures on the western face with a lesser number on the opposite side. As is usual with the Coso concentrations, most of the designs occur where the gorge begins. There are a number of hunting blinds near the drawings, and of particular interest are the dummy figures made of piled-up stones to simulate hunters that line the top of the cliffs on the east side. A number of chipping areas occur on the benches along the arroyo and there is a large occupation cave. Sheep, shield patterns, and decorated anthropomorphs predominate. Total designs—1174.

Blind at (Iny-42). (Emory Strong photo.)

Two Bowmen Apparently Shooting at One Another (R-25).

(R-35).

Unknown Objects With Ceremonial Figure (Iny-8F).

(R-26).

Double- and Single-Weighted Atlatls, Types 1 and 2 (R-25).

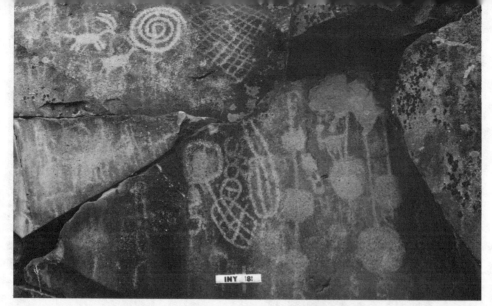

This Panel Shows an Atlatl With Three Stones (R-35).

(R-25).

Every Animal on This Panel Is Impaled by an Arrow or Spear (R-26).

Some Curious Motifs That Look Something Like Handbags. Note the animal tracks (R-25).

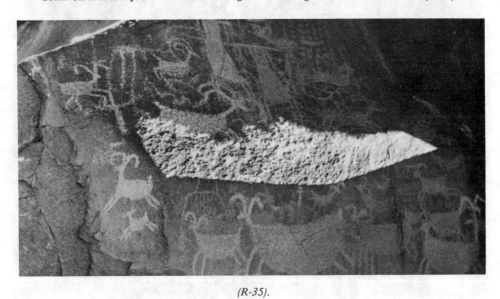

(R-35).

A Deer and Many Sheep. The deer is rare in the Coso Range (R-35).

The Decoration of Rock Edge Is Unusual (R-25).

Deeply Pecked and Incised Designs. The rock faces down-canyon and shows extensive sandblasting (R-25).

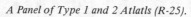

A Panel of Type 1 and 2 Atlatls (R-25).

(R-26).

A Deeply Pecked Design From the Section of Renegade Canyon Believed To Have the Oldest Drawings (R-25).

(R-26).

Notice the Wind Erosion on Lower Parts of This Panel. During much of the year, Wind-blown sand scours the bottom 10 feet of the canyons severely (R-35).

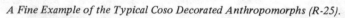

A Fine Example of the Typical Coso Decorated Anthropomorphs (R-25).

Note Sheephorn Headdresses In Lower Right (R-35).

Large Ceremonial Figure Holding Single Rod and Three Short Rods (Bow and Arrows?). This combination is common in the area (R-25).

87

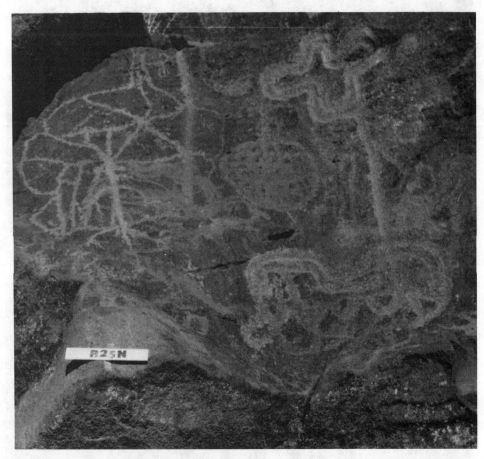

Deeply Pecked Abstract Patterns. These are among the earliest drawings in the Coso Range (R-25).

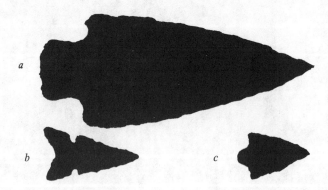

Three projectile points from the Renegade Canyon area. a. Atlatl dart point. b. c. Arrow points. All of obsidian. Actual size.

9. THE SURROUNDING MINOR SITES

The highest development of the rock art in the Coso region is localized in three canyons: Petroglyph Canyon, its large tributary, Sheep Canyon, and Renegade Canyon. Certain characteristic Coso elements such as sheep with horns to the front, the weighted atlatl, elaborate anthropomorphs, and the shield-like patterns occur sparingly at many outlying sites, but the workmanship with rare exceptions is quite crude. Most of the minor sites are small, averaging about 150 elements, but a few, such as Iny-39 near Coso Hot Springs, are very large with over 1000 designs . Perhaps the most interesting of the surrounding sites are those that lie around Little Lake. In Pluvial times, this lake was fed by a river spilling over the height of land from Owens Lake. Later a small lake was kept alive through springs, and in the historic period the lake was enlarged by means of an earth dam at the lower end. For many thousands of years, aboriginal populations were attracted to the area. There were people who lived here part or all of the year and others who stopped here while passing through the country. This accounts for the extraordinary diversity of rock art around the Lake. At least three basically different styles are found here side by side.

The pecked designs, especially at the northernmost sites, are mainly Great Basin Curvilinear Abstract and are probably the earliest Little Lake type. With them are sheep with horns to the side, drawn in the characteristic crude Owens Valley manner. At the lower end of Iny-26, there is a large concentration of Coso type atlatls and a few sheep with horns front. On the western side of the lake among the rock pecked drawings, there are two areas of paintings that appear very late and typical of the Kawaiisu and Tubatulabal rock paintings to the southeast. At the largest site on the southern end of the Lake, all three styles occur together.

West of Coso Hot Springs, there is a site of paintings (Iny-1) on a granite surface that includes "pelt" figures, so common in the Kern River region and in the San Joaquin Valley. At the same site, deer are painted with boat-shaped bodies reminiscent of the boat-shaped sheep from Petroglyph Canyon.

There are two caves in the Renegade Canyon drainage that depict crude human and abstract figures in red and orange; they are late prehistoric and utterly unlike the Coso rock engravings.

Iny-1 Pumice Mine

This site is located on a tremendous granite rock near an open pit pumice mine. Turn off Highway 14 at Coso Junction and drive about 4 miles east to dirt road on left; take this road about 4 miles to pumice mine, then west 1/4 mile to site. The paintings in red, black and white are badly eroded. The subject matter is naturalisitc—sheep, deer, humans, hands, etc. Design elements—approximately 25. (See discussion under "Walker Pass—Kern River.")

Iny-2 Haiwee Springs No. 1

Take the jeep track leading northwest from Coso Hot Springs. After approximately 5 miles, the road dead-ends at Haiwee Springs, one of the better springs in the region. There were several thousand chukar partridge at the springs when we recorded the site in September. A dense growth of willows half a mile long marks the water in the canyon bottom. Most of the rock drawings are located on boulders high above the streambed. The workmanship is very crude and the subject matter confined to sheep and curvilinear abstract patterns. Design elements—about 50.

Haiwee Springs. One of the largest springs in the Coso Range. The willows in the canyon floor mark the extent of the water. In the fall, immense numbers of chukar partridge and quail gather here.

Iny-3 Junction Ranch No. 1

The site is on both sides of the road in a short narrow gorge, 1/2 mile west of the junction of the Etcheron Valley road and the Coso Hot Springs Road. Design elements—about 20, mainly abstract.

Iny-4 Junction Ranch No. 2

The site is located 3/4 of a mile south of Junction Ranch on a low basaltic outcrop to the west of the road. The design elements are sheep and abstract patterns—about 20.

Iny-5 Junction Ranch No. 3

This large site is 2 1/2 miles north of Junction Ranch on low cliffs bordering the west side of a wash to the west of the road. The drawings are well executed and depict most of the elements seen at the major sites. These include elaborate anthropomorphs, sheep, shield patterns, dogs, snakes, and projectile points. A curious motif concentrated at this site and with single examples at Iny-8B and Iny-43 is an anthropomorphic figure with tanged projectile points attached to his head or shoulders. Approximate number—450.

Iny-5A Junction Ranch No. 4

Scattered on small boulders 200 yards southwest of Junction Ranch are a number of abstract and sheep rock drawings of poor quality. There are house rings, metates and a hunting blind nearby. About 20 designs.

Iny-6 Millspaugh Site

One mile east of the Etcheron Valley road on the Millspaugh road. The site is at the base of a 400-foot escarpment on the south side of the road and the drawings occur on isolated boulders. The workmanship is only fair and design elements include sheep, shield patterns, horned anthropomorphs, snakes and lines of stick figures. About 100 elements.

Iny-11 Darwin Wash

A unique site for the area—pecked drawings on granitic rock (Adamilite). Six and one-half miles north of Junction Ranch, the Darwin road takes a 90-degree turn west and crosses Darwin Wash. On the west side of the wash, the road again turns north. At this point the site is visible several hundred yards to the west of the road—two very large granitic boulders about 20 feet high. The patina on the rocks is a light brown type and the roughly pecked drawings are difficult to photograph. The designs, numbering about 100, include sheep, solid-body anthropomorphs, tracks, birds, and miscellaneous abstract patterns.

Iny-12 Linnie Site

Across Highway 14 from the Nine Mile Canyon road is a short road that dead-ends at the Southern Pacific Railway tracks. Beyond the tracks and 1/2 mile inside the Naval Weapons Center boundary, a wide shallow wash narrows and drops off 20 feet into a wide box canyon. This box canyon, open at the south to Indian Wells Valley, would have made a perfect antelope corral and was doubtless used for this purpose. This is on the ancient waterway that took the overflow from Owens Lake into the China Lake Basin. Around the horseshoe-shaped upper end of the canyon, there are rock drawings of fair quality, mainly sheep with a few deer, dogs, and abstracts. About 35 elements.

Iny-13 Upper Centennial Spring

This is the most northerly site in the Coso Range. From Junction Ranch, drive to the turnoff to Petroglyph Canyon (see Iny-7). Continue on for 6 1/2 miles to Coles Spring (large square concrete tank) where road starts to climb sharply toward Coso Peak. The country changes character at about 7000 feet, where the sage and Joshua tree environment gives way to stands of Piñon pine and some large specimens of California juniper. Three miles beyond Coles Spring at elevation 7600, take the left fork (through locked gate). The road now drops down through Centennial Flat and after 8 miles the north boundary of the Base is crossed at Iny-14. At next road fork (1/2 mile), take right road down canyon (1/2 mile) to round concrete tank and corral. The drawings are concentrated on the hillside above and east of the spring, but scattered designs occur up the draw above the springs with bedrock mortars in the bottom of the draw. These mortars and a few at R-25 and R-8 in Renegade Canyon are the only examples in the Coso Range that we saw during the survey. By contrast, many thousands of bedrock milling stones or metates were noted. This is a big site with several hundred elements.

Iny-14 Upper Centennial Flat

This site is about 1/2 mile south of Iny-13 and exactly on the north NWC boundary. It occupies two small gorges that form the head of the canyon. There are many dim abstract patterns and solid-body anthropomorphs; all look old. There are approximately 100 design elements.

Iny-15 Coso Peak No. 1

From Iny-18, take right fork to the north (Coso Peak Road). At 1/2 mile there is a locked gate. Beyond the gate a short distance there is a fork; take left for 1/2 mile to triple fork; take left fork to rocky promontory. The site is at the bottom of the southeast face. There are 16 rectilinear abstract designs and one sheep.

Iny-16 Coso Peak No. 2

Two miles down grade from Iny-18 on the Centennial Flat Road, there is a large basaltic outcrop to the left and near the road. This site is located by a number of very large juniper trees and includes well-executed Transitional and Late design elements. There are 3 caves here including a tunnel-like cave with 3 medicine bags pecked in the rock at the inner end. A hunting blind is located against the cliff. Approximate number of design elements—150.

Iny-17 Coso Peak No. 3

This is a small site with only one panel to the left of the road and 1 mile west of Iny-16. Two atlatls; two abstract designs.

Piñon Forest Near Coso Peak. Iny-19 in center of picture.

Iny-18 Coso Peak No. 4

Three miles northwest of Coles Spring near junction with Centennial Flat Road. There are scattered drawings on both sides of the road for about 1/4 of a mile. This area is relatively unexplored. There is an immense amount of basaltic rock above the 7000-mile level and only sites near the roads have been surveyed. About 300 design elements.

Iny-19 Coso Peak No. 5

Southwest of Iny-18 along the face of the basaltic escarpment, there are scattered sites—some with a dozen or so designs, others with only one or two. In all, we recorded five rock masses with drawings in a 2-mile stretch, mainly abstract with a few sheep. Total drawings—about 60.

Iny-20 Airport Lake

This small site is located about 17 miles northwest of China Lake and at the northern tip of Airport Lake. There is a locked security gate a mile south of the site. The site is on several large boulders at the base of a large lava flow. There is a cave and house rings nearby. This is the lowest in altitude of any of the Coso sites (2400 feet). There are about 25 sheep and stick figures in single file.

Iny-21 Wilson Canyon

Take the road up Wilson Canyon (turn right off the main China Lake-Darwin Road about 11 1/2 miles north of China Lake, main gate). The site is at a basalt flow that crosses the canyon about 5 miles from the turn-off. The drawings are on cliffs on either side of the road. These are very crude pictures and may well be the work of the Desert Kawaiisu whose territory adjoins that of the Western Shoshoni in this area. Design elements—about 100.

Iny-23 Little Lake No. 1

This side includes the entire west side of Little Lake where low basalt cliffs line the shore. This site is most easily seen by boat. The intermittent pecked designs include elements from all Coso Periods but no atlatls. At two small spots near the two northernmost coves, there are abstract paintings. One is in a protected spot and is painted in polychrome—red, black, and white. The patterns are utterly unlike the Coso Range or the Owens Valley style and resemble the paintings from the Tehachapi Mountains and the Kern River area. Pecked elements—about 400; painted elements—11.

Iny-24 Stahl Site

This site is in a rock shelter in an isolated outcrop of lava, 1/2 mile northwest of the upper end of Little Lake. This site was excavated and described by M. R. Harrington (1957). There are a few crude sheep and humans pecked and scratched on the rear wall.

Iny-25 Little Lake No. 2

This is the most extensive site at Little Lake including a considerable part of the cliff at the southeast end of the lake and a few scattered designs along the water (some are under water; the lake level has been artifically raised a few feet by an earth dam). Most of the designs are pecked with Coso type drawings and Great Basin Abstract patterns. Sheep are rare and there are no atlatls. At ground level, there are four spots where paintings in red occur. They are rectilinear abstractions unlike anything in the region. They are on exposed surfaces and must be late. In a number of instances traces of red paint can be seen on the lines of earlier rock engravings. About 500 pecked designs; 7 painted. (For additional information on the painted designs here and at Iny-23, see "Walker Pass—Kern River" section.)

Iny-26 Atlatl Cliff

One-quarter mile north of Little Lake and east of the dry stream bed, there is a decorated area about 600 yards long. The designs occur on the large tumbled basalt rocks to a height of over 75 feet. There are sheep, bear tracks and abstract patterns, but the most interesting motif is the atlatl. It is the most abundant element at the site (over 30) and the only concentration of the weapon outside the Petroglyph-Renegade Canyon area. Other elements—about 100.

Iny-27 Grant Mesa No. 1

Site is reached by walking west by north from main site at Iny-7A for about a mile. After crossing Horse Canyon, the mesa rises gently to the west. The drawings are scattered on small boulders over about 2 acres of land. Designs indicate this is a Late site. About 75 design elements.

Iny-28 Grant Mesa No. 2

About 1/4 mile south of Iny-27, there is another site very similar in size and appearance. About 50 elements.

Iny-29 Grant Mesa No. 3

One-third mile west of Iny-27, a high scarp drops off over 1,000 feet into the next canyon west. At the top of the cliff are a few Late type sheep.

Iny-30 Birchim Spring No. 1

At the top of Mountain Springs Canyon, take the road turning off to the southeast; at 1/2 mile take left fork; at 1/2 mile take another left fork; at 1/2 mile take right fork to old house. The site is about 500 feet up the draw and 150 feet up the opposite hillside. The workmanship is poor. About 500 elements.

Iny-31 Birchim Spring No. 2

Follow road northeast from Iny-30 for about 1 mile. Where road turns southeast, walk up slope to north to small site (two panels of abstract patterns) on low dike. About 20 elements.

Iny-32 Renegade Grade

At the junction of the Renegade Canyon-Mountain Springs Roads, take left-hand road. About 4 miles up the grade, there is an abrupt hairpin turn, first to the left and then to the right. At the next turn, there is a large mass of rock on the left near the road. The designs are deer, sheep, quail and anthropomorphic figures—about 80. The deer here are in fair numbers (perhaps a half dozen and one is double ended).

Iny-33 Ruby Spring No. 1

From Iny-31, continue southeast over jeep track for 1 1/2 miles to edge of mesa where land drops off abruptly toward Searles Basin. Ruby Spring lies about a mile to the east of Iny-33 and 500 feet lower. The site is on two groups of boulders on the edge of the drop-off. Workmanship is very crude (sheep hardly recognizable); much curvilinear abstract and pit-and-groove that is either Late or reworked. Approximately 200 elements.

Iny-34 Ruby Spring No. 2

Northeast of Iny-33 about 1/4 mile is a group of small sites that occur from outcrop to outcrop to the major unit, a commanding high point at the southeast and where the mesa narrows to a waist only a few yards wide. The workmanship and subject matter are similar to Iny-33; there are some sheep with horns coming from body—no head. About 200 elements.

Iny-35 Divide No. 1

From the Renegade Canyon parking area drive north on jeep track along east side of canyon for about 1 mile. Then cross arroyo to the west and ascend gentle slope 1/4 mile. The site is on a small outcropping of basalt to the left of the road. Designs, mainly sheep with some dogs and shields, total about 100.

Iny-36 Divide No. 2

About 1/2 mile farther up the grade from Iny-35, there is a sizable mass of basalt to the right and near the road. Designs similar to Iny-35—about 90 elements.

Iny-37 Ross Cave

This site is located 2 miles northeast of the parking area at Renegade Canyon and in a cave 1/4 mile south of the road. There are two circular abstract designs, one in red and the other in orange.

Iny-38 Coso Wash

Six miles northeast of Coso Hot Springs on very rough Coso Hot Springs-Junction Ranch Road. A few pecked drawings on boulders in wash 200 feet from road. Nearby is the largest number of house rings noted in the Coso survey—14. About 20 elements.

Iny-39 Gill Site

From Coso Hot Springs, drive 1 1/2 miles on the jeep road to Haiwee Springs. Take dim track to right 1/2 mile to bad arroyo crossing, then 2 miles along hogback to where road drops down onto mesa. The site stretches along a basaltic cliff for 3/4 mile. This is an important site with workmanship fair to good. Many sheep and anthropomorphs with miscellaneous abstractions, but no atlatls. About 1,000 designs.

Iny-40 Black Canyon

About halfway between Coso Hot Springs and Iny-38, a narrow flat on the south side of the road marks the head of Black Canyon. The site is a 500-yard section of the cliffs on the west side of this flat. Atlatls, sheep, and abstracts are the principal subjects. There are house rings on the flat nearby. Total elements—112.

Iny-41 Carricut Lake No. 1

One-half mile south of Carricut Lake (dry) and 3 miles south of Junction Ranch, there is a lava cliff about 1/2 mile long. Iny-41 covers 200 yards of the northeast end. Designs include sheep, shield patterns and atlatls and miscellaneous abstract. About 100 elements.

Iny-41A Carricut Lake No. 2

This site is located at the southwest end of the cliff described for Iny-41. The designs are similar and number about 150.

Iny-42 Carricut Lake No. 3

This site is 1 mile south of Iny-41 following a jeep track along the base of the mountain. There is a malpais formation west of the road with scattered groups of drawings near three hunting blinds. Drawings of sheep, medicine bags, shield patterns, etc., occur all around cliffs for over 1/2 mile. About 150 elements.

Iny-43 Parrish Gorge

One mile northwest of Junction Ranch, a narrow basalt gorge enters the upper end of Darwin Wash. The designs, including sheep, bowmen, atlatls, and anthropomorphs, are concentrated at the entrance to the gorge. A hunting blind is located not far above this point. About 250 elements.

Atlatls at a Little Lake Site (Iny-26).

Ceremonial Figures Highly Simplified. They have only rudimentary arms or none and are lacking feet (Iny-39).

Barely Recognizeable Sheep From an Argus Range Site (Iny-34).

The Head-to-tail Arrangement Is Unusual (Iny-16).

98

The Raised Lake Level Has Destroyed the Patina. Many drawings are under water when the lake is full (Iny-25).

(Iny-34).

This Site Had the Most Primitive Patterns in the Area (Iny-34).

These Designs Are Characteristic of the Great Basin Rectilinear Style (Iny-39).

The Sheep With Reverse Horns Is Unusual. There is only one other example (Iny-16).

Part of a Large Site Near Junction Ranch (Iny-43).

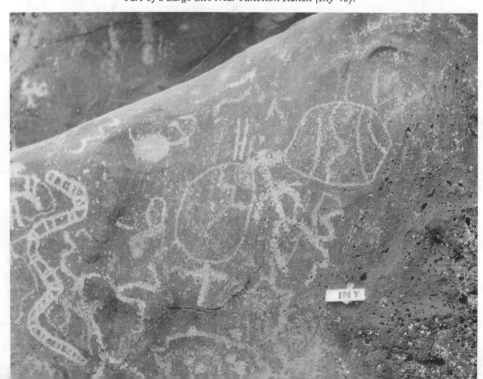

Crudely Pecked Patterns on a Rough Basalt (Iny-33).

The Spiral Is an Unusual Design in the Coso Region (Iny-26).

(Iny-42).

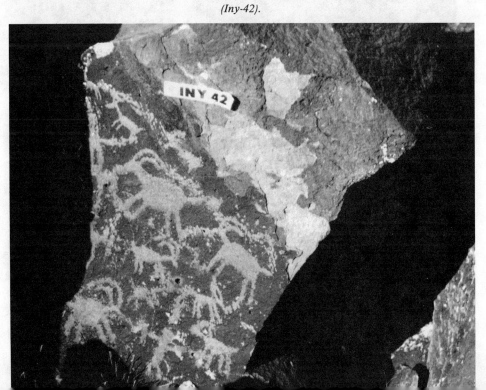

Anthropomorph With Projectile Headdress (Iny-5).

(R-23).

TABLE 3. Coso Site Locations on U.S. Geological Survey Maps.

Site	Map	Location	Elevation	Site	Map	Location	Elevation
Iny-1	Haiwee Reservoir	T21S-R38E-S14	5080	Iny-14	Coso Peak	T19S-R39E-S32	6400
Iny-2	Haiwee Reservoir	T21S-R39E-S10	4800	Iny-15	Coso Peak	T20S-R35E-S15	7500
Iny-3	Coso Peak	T22S-R41E-S2	6000	Iny-16	Coso Peak	T22S-R35E-S21	7000
Iny-4	Coso Peak	T21S-R41E-S35	5800	Iny-17	Coso Peak	T22S-R35E-S21	6800
Iny-5	Coso Peak	T21S-R41E-S15	5300	Iny-18	Coso Peak	T22S-R39E-S25	7600
Iny-5A	Coso Peak	T21S-R41E-S35	5720	Iny-19	Coso Peak	T20S-R39E-S26-34	6900-7500
Iny-6	Maturango Peak	T22S-R41E-S6	6000	Iny-20	Little Lake	T22S-R39E-S21	2400
Iny-7	Coso Peak	T22S-R40E-S4	5200	Iny-21	Mountain Springs	T24S-R41E-S10	4000
Iny-7A	Coso Peak	T22S-R40E-S9	5160	Iny-23	Little Lake	T22S-R38E-S8	3200
Iny-7B	Coso Peak	T22S-T40E-S8	4800	Iny-24	Little Lake	T22S-R38E-S6	3200
Iny-7C	Coso Peak	T22S-R40E-S20	5200	Iny-25	Little Lake	T22S-R38E-S8	3200
Iny-7D	Coso Peak	T22S-R40E-S4	5400	Iny-26	Little Lake	T22S-R38E-S5	3200
Iny-8	Coso Peak	T22S-R40E-S13	5400	Iny-27	Coso Peak	T22S-R40E-S5	5400
Iny-8A	Coso Peak	T22S-R40E-S24	5080	Iny-28	Coso Peak	T22S-R40E-S5	5300
Iny-8B	Mountain Springs	T22S-R40E-S25	4800-5000	Iny-29	Coso Peak	T22S-R40E-S5	5480
Iny-8C	Coso Peak	T22S-R40E-S24	5080	Iny-30	Trona	T23S-R42E-S17	5600
Iny-8D	Mountain Springs	T22S-R40E-S26	4840	Iny-31	Trona	T23S-R42E-S9	5480
Iny-8E	Coso Peak	T22S-R40E-S23	5200	Iny-32	Mountain Springs	T23S-R40E-S2	3900
Iny-8F	Coso Peak	T22S-R41E-S8	5600	Iny-33	Trona	T23S-R42E-S21	5360
Iny-9	Coso Peak	T22S-R40E-S10	5200	Iny-34	Trona	T22S-R42E-S19-21-22	5260-5360
Iny-9A	Coso Peak	T22S-R40E-S15	5120	Iny-35	Coso Peak	T22S-R40E-S13	5200
Iny-9B	Coso Peak	T22S-R40E-S16	4800-5000	Iny-36	Coso Peak	T22S-R40E-S14	5400
Iny-9C	Coso Peak	T22S-R40E-S17	4600	Iny-37	Mountain Springs	T22S-R41E-S28	5400
Iny-9D	Coso Peak	T22S-R40E-S20	4200-4400	Iny-38	Coso Peak	T21S-R40E-S20	5600
Iny-9E	Coso Peak	T22S-R40E-S12	5600	Iny-39	Coso Peak	T21S-R39E-S26-35	4200
Iny-9F	Coso Peak	T22S-R40E-S13	5400	Iny-40	Coso Peak	T22S-R39E-S1	4400
Iny-10	Coso Peak	T22S-R40E-S8	4800-5000	Iny-41	Maturango Peak	T22S-R41E-S7	5680
Iny-11	Coso Peak	T20S-R41E-S29	4600	Iny-41A	Maturango Peak	T22S-R41E-S7	5680
Iny-12	Little Lake	T24S-R38E-S22	2600	Iny-42	Maturango Peak	T22S-R41E-S18	5700
Iny-13	Coso Peak	T19S-R39E-S32	6400	Iny-43	Coso Peak	T21S-R41E-S27	5400-5500

10. RELATIONSHIPS WITH ADJOINING AREAS

It would be reasonable to assume that the distinctive style developed in the Coso Range would have a marked influence on the rock art of the immediately adjoining regions. Such, however, is not the case. Subject matter connected with the Transitional and Late Periods, such as the elaborate patterned-body anthropomorphs, dogs, processions of figures, and medicine bags, is highly localized even in the Coso Range itself. This chapter will trace outside influences on the Coso style and the effect of this style on the adjacent Shoshonean peoples.

OWENS VALLEY

Owens Valley, lying directly north of the Coso Range, is flanked on the west by the Sierra Nevada and on the east by the White and Inyo Mountains. Its northern limit is near Birchim Canyon a few miles above Bishop where the land rises sharply for several thousands of feet. Its southern limit is the Coso Range.

Until the diversion of the Owens River to supply water to Los Angeles, the valley was well watered for its entire length and in prehistoric times supported a large population. These were the Owens Valley Paiute, a Shonshonean-speaking people. A sizable remnant of these Indians (about 1,200, Kroeber, 1925), still live around the towns in the northern half of the valley, above the aqueduct intake.

The valley shows evidence of much volcanic activity for its entire length, and there is an abundance of rock engravings as well as a few painted sites. Von Werlhof (1925) has done a thorough survey of the Owens Valley rock art, and his report shows that the designs are overwhelmingly of the Great Basin Abstract type described by Steward (1929), and Heizer and Baumhoff (1962). Occasionally there are drawings of sheep and deer that can be compared with the crudest examples from the Coso region. None of the Owens Valley sheep are drawn with horns to the front, so characteristic of the Coso region. The only typical Coso element we have been able to find in the valley is a single Type 1 atlatl on a limestone outcrop near Keeler (northeast edge of Owens Lake), and not far from the Coso Range.

On the other hand, the earliest Coso drawings show a definite Great Basin Abstract influence, an influence that in all likelihood came from the north. There is a juxtaposition at Little Lake of Great Basin Curvilinear elements with a large concentration of Type 1 and 2 atlatls.

Owens Valley Design Elements. a. Chalfant Valley, Mono County. b. Chalk Bluffs near Bishop. c. The most elaborate of the Owens Valley panels (21 feet long) Casa Diablo tableland near Bishop. d. Chalk Bluffs. e. Poverty Hills near Aberdeen, Mono County. f. Fish Slough north of Bishop. c. from photo by John Cawley, all others after von Werlhof, (1955).

DEATH VALLEY

The northern section of Death Valley was occupied in historic times by Western Shoshoni people identical with those living in the Coso and Argus ranges to the west. In the southern part of the valley, the Kawaiisu were the dominant people with a certain number of Western Shoshoni and Chemehuevi. Lack of water was a critical factor in this harshest of environments and the population at the start of the first white contact has been estimated at less than 50 (Steward, 1938).

Only one Death Valley site shows definite Coso influence. This is in Greenwater Canyon in the southeastern section of the valley. At this site, there are 19 atlatls of Type 1 and they appear to be among the oldest drawings in the locality. Sheep occur at 22 of the Death Valley sites. They are invariably of the horns-to-the-side type and the workmanship is usually quite crude. Only one location high in the Panamints is recognizably in the Great Basin Abstract style. There are many light-colored rocks in the valley and simple abstract patterns; deer, sheep and phallic stick-men are painted at a number of sites in white, red and black.

In the Coso Range and in the adjoining Argus Range, the engravings occur on a single type of rock, basaltic lava. The Death Valley rock drawings (actually located in the Panamint Range on the west side and the Amargosa Range on the east) are found on a great variety of rocks reflecting the complex mineralization of the region. The principal rocks utilized by the prehistoric engravers and painters were basalt, limestone, monzanite, rhyolite, quartzite, sandstone, siltstone, and tuff.

The situation in Death Valley and its surrounding ranges reflects occasional outside influence (possibly the result of sporadic seed-gathering or hunting by people from the Coso and Owens Valley regions). The rock pictures of the Death Valley Indians never achieved anything approaching the excellence or the variety of the Coso Range rock art. The subjects include designs based on elaborations of the circle, spirals, shield-like patterns, and miscellaneous abstracts. The motivation was certainly the same as in the Coso and Owens Valley areas—hunting magic. There is one instance of a thunderbird in Death Valley almost identical with three in the Coso area. These examples are uncharacteristic of eastern California rock art and show influences from the southwest.

There are a few sites in the Saline Range between the Inyo Mountains and the Panamint Range that feature Great Basin abstract patterns and horns-to-the-side sheep.

This section is based on the work done in Death Valley by Donald Martin of Santa Rosa. Over a period of nearly 20 years, he has recorded 74 sites in or near the Monument.

WALKER PASS—KERN RIVER

Walker Pass (5250 feet) cuts through the southern end of the Sierra Nevada 16 miles west of China Lake (35 air miles southwest of Petroglyph Canyon). This pass is the gateway to the Kern River and the lower San Joaquin Valley. The Kern River and its main tributary,

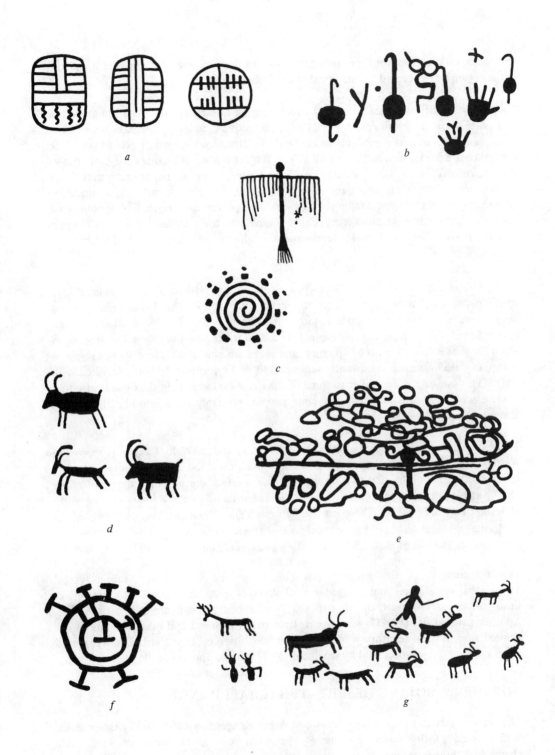

Death Valley Design Elements. a. Greenwater Canyon No. 2. b. Greenwater Canyon No. 1. c. Marble Canyon. d. Emigrant Canyon. e. Paleomesa. f. Arrastre Spring. g. Greenwater Canyon, a painting in red, black, and white. (All drawings from photographs by Don Martin.)

the south fork of the Kern, are the major streams draining the southern Sierra and the entire region was occupied by the Shoshonean Tubatulabal.

Their rock art differs radically from the rock engraved designs of the Coso Range. In the first place, most of the designs are painted, a technique dictated by the basic rock of the area, granite. Granite is a medium to light-colored stone and incised or pecked lines lack the contrast essential for picture making. The subject matter, with one exception, shows no influence from the Great Basin side of the Sierra. Some of the common motifs are spoked wheels, "pelt" figures painted with single or polychrome outlines, semicircular designs, rayed circles, and phallic stick-figures. The polychrome style, first encountered with the Tubatulabal, becomes increasingly complex to the west among the San Joaquin Yokuts and reaches its ultimate development in the coastal ranges with the Chumash Indians.

There is one site on the Kern River just south of Lake Isabella that is *pecked* into lightly-patinated granite. The subject matter is quite unlike the Tubatulabal painted designs and the entire site appears quite old. The designs are Type 1 atlatls, circles, bisected circles, and dots. Those designs that are on rocks near the splash line of summer water flow have lost all contrast—pictures and rocks are blue-black. Here is an example of optimum patina-forming conditions: super-heated rocks continually being splashed with water. This one site is so similar to some of the Early Period sites in the Coso Range that it seems certain it was made by the same people, probably on a hunting trip in Kern Canyon.

There is a site on the eastern slope of the Sierra in Indian Wells Canyon (supposedly Western Shoshoni territory) that is painted in polychrome and includes grids, concentric circles, anthropomorphs, and two horsemen. This is a late site probably dating from the 1860's and, though the technique suggests the Tubatulabal or the Kawaiisu to the south of Walker Pass, it might have been made by Owens Valley Paiute or Western Shoshoni. At Little Lake there are two Painted sites of abstract patterns, some of which are in polychrome. The use of multiple color outlining suggests Tubatulabal origin.

The westernmost of the painted sites (Iny-1) in the Coso Range shows typical Tubatulabal pelt figures and some deer and sheep in red, black and white that reflect Coso influence. These are on an exposed granite boulder and are still fairly visible. Another painted site (Iny-37) has two abstract patterns in red and orange. Some of the painted sites in Coso territory were possibly made during or after the Indian war period when the country was occupied by small bands of homeless Indians on the move.

NORTHERN MOJAVE DESERT—TEHACHAPI RANGE

The Mojave Desert south of the Coso and Argus Ranges is a conspicuously inhospitable land, a land of dry lakes and sparse vegetation, low, stony mountain ranges and abandoned mining camps. It was the territory of the Kawaiisu, another Shoshonean group. These people ranged nearly as far west as the Kern River and occupied the mountains where the southern Sierra Nevada meets the Tehachapi Range. To the east, their land included the southern halves of Panamint and Death Valleys.

Kern River–Walker Pass Design Elements. a and b. Polchrome painting in red, black, and white, Kern River at Erskine Creek. c. Painting in red, Cane Springs, Greenhorn Range. d. The only rock-carved site in the region, Kern River at Isabella Dam. e. Painting in red, Kelso Valley. f. Painting in red, Canebrake Creek near Walker Pass. (c and f from photographs by Robert Luthy.)

Northern Mojave Desert—Tehachapi Range Design Elements. a. Painting in red, black, white, and green. Horse Canyon, Tehachapi Range. b. Painting in red, black, and white, Jawbone Canyon, southern Sierra Nevada. c and g. Black Canyon near Hinkley. d. Painting in red and white on black, Tylerhorse Canyon, Tehachapi Range. e. Steam Wells near Randsburg. f. Inscription Canyon near Hinkley. h. Sheep Springs near Randsburg. (b, c, d, e, and h from photographs by John Cawler, g. Black Canyon near Hinkley, f after Gruber, 1961.)

This region was thinly populated and the rock art sites are equally few and scattered. The nearest sites to the Coso region are in the mountains northwest and southwest of Randsburg. The former at Sheep Springs, Steam Wells and Goler Canyon are basically Great Basin Curvilinear in style. The only typical Coso elements are sheep, sheep horns and several Type 1 atlatls at one site. The affinity would be with the Early Period of the Coso Range. The sites southeast of Randsburg are in Black Canyon and Inscription Canyon where the predominant style is the Great Basin Rectilinear with a few sheep of the horns-to-the-side type. The rare thunderbird motif occurs once in this area.

The rock art of the western part of the Kawaiisu range is so different that it seems improbable that it was made by the same people. Here the country rock is granite and the pecked and abraded technique gives way to a painted technique. The style is similar to that of the Kern River Tubatulabal and the lower San Joaquin Yokuts with whom the late prehistoric and historic Kawaiisu must have maintained close ties. Pelt figures, centipedes, and spoked wheels are common as is the use of polychrome outlining of figures. These paintings of the Tehachapi-Sierra Nevada mountains appear late, while most of the desert region rock engravings are certainly much older.

This summary of the adjoining areas indicates how highly localized was the phenomenon of the Coso rock art. The only major outside influence, the wide-spread Great Basin Abstract, triggered the start of the Coso rock engraving period which then developed quite independently. We believe this development was mainly due to the unique geological formations of the region, ideal for the systematic and continuous hunting of the bighorn sheep.

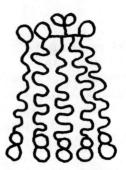

11. CONCLUSIONS

Based on our Coso research, much reading of Great Basin studies, and a generous amount of speculation, the picture begins to look like this.

By at least 8,000 years ago, small groups of people were living in the Great Basin with the atlatl and the milling stone as the two basic cultural items. They were mainly living near or along the edges of the large Pleistocene lakes created by the Great Pluvial that ended the last ice age. Lithic evidence of this has been recovered in open sites, while perishable evidence has been excavated from caves in the foothills and in the mountains.

As the years passed, the environment began to change. The land became progressively hotter and dryer and the various Indian groups moved from one area to another, either voluntarily or by displacement by aggressive newcomers. The lakes shrank and many disappeared. What had been chiefly a lacustrine culture became increasingly a desert-oriented culture. The physical objects that have been preserved, however, demonstrate a remarkable homogeneity throughout the Great Basin. The atlatl, the milling stone, and basketry tell the story of people leading a simple seed-gathering and hunting life. As the land dried up, there was doubtless a tendency for family groups to seek higher land where permanent water in the form of springs or streams occurred.

The drying out of the land was arrested 3,000 to 4,000 years ago by another rainy period, the Little Pluvial, that replenished the dead or dying Pleistocene lakes, allowing for another period of lake-oriented life by the Great Basin Indians.

Our first solid evidence that man was living in the Coso region comes from this era. Harrington's excavations at Little Lake show that man was living in caves and in houses there at least 3,000 years ago. Glottochronology studies indicate that the Numic or Plateau Shoshoneans occupied the region at this time and that the Coso Range was part of the original Shoshonean "heartland" (southeastern California and southern Nevada) from which they later emigrated to occupy the entire Great Basin and the Colorado Plateau.

It is not possible to say just when or why the first rock drawings were made in the Coso area, but one can theorize that the first abstract designs were created by the ancestors of the Numic Shoshoneans moving into the region from the north. The dark patination of rocks, necessary for the creation of pecked and abraded designs, appears to depend on the action of simultaneous heat and water that can occur only during summer thundershowers. Prolonged cold, wet periods tend to inhibit and destroy patina. Thus the patina formed during the Altithermal or drying period following the Great Pluvial might have been destroyed by the Little Pluvial, and the patina we see today would have formed *since* the Little Pluvial. Thus it is possible that no drawings in the Coso Range are much over 3,000 years old.

In any case, the picture 3,000 years ago in the Coso Range was something like this. Small family groups and groups of family groups were leading a basically seed-gathering existence augmented with atlatl hunting (chiefly of sheep, deer and antelope) with some fishing in nearby lakes and streams (Owens Lake, Sierra Nevada) and seasonal taking of waterfowl.

Of the animals hunted, the most highly prized was the bighorn sheep, a large animal with excellent flesh and hide. The bighorn was also the most difficult to take. A herding animal, it is easily alarmed and takes refuge in rough, inaccessible terrain. The atlatl dart, slow moving and only truly effective at short range, apparently did not make large kills possible. As a result, the large bands that occupied the region at that time were not decimated.

At some early period the practice of picturing the bighorn on rocks was introduced, an outgrowth of the more ancient practice of making nonrepresentational or abstract designs on rocks. Whether this began as a depiction of the animals killed or animals *to be killed*, we do not know, but it is our belief that most of the immense number of sheep drawings were connected with hunting magic—the drawing of the sought-after animal would help bring the hunter success.

It is very likely that during this early time, the Shoshoneans had about as meager a ceremonial life as their descendants, the historical Shoshoneans. Something new, however, was about to come into the area that would have a tremendous impact on these people.

Sometime between 1000 B.C. and A.D. 1 the bow and arrow was introduced. Its appearance is graphically shown on the rock panels and boulders in the Coso Range. The drawings of weighted atlatls and crudely made sheep gradually give way to archers, highly stylized sheep, and elaborate ceremonial figures.

The bow ushered in the highest development of the Coso rock art and the number of drawings from the Transitional and Late Periods in a relatively small area is almost unbelievable. To account for this flowering of rock art, the rise and decline of ceremonialism, and the end to the rock drawing tradition, we have theorized that somthing like this occurred.

The bow truly revolutionized the killing of game, particularly the bighorn sheep. The swift arrow, launched from the ambush blinds without the necessity of standing up to cast the atlatl dart, made killing easier and also possible at longer ranges. Advanced hunting techniques, employing dogs for driving game, utilizing every possible migration route open to the sheep for ambushing, and the use of a growing population for larger and larger communal hunts, made killing on a large scale possible. For a time, the sheep probably became the most important food source and the economy of the people revolved around its capture, much as the Northwest Indian culture depended on the salmon and the Plains Indians relied heavily on the buffalo.

Both the salmon and the buffalo became the objects of ceremonial veneration and we think the same thing occurred in the Coso area. The new ease of taking the game probably had the effect of making hunting magic of secondary importance to the ritual picturing of the bighorn to assure his favor and continued appearance to be killed. How long this period of relative prosperity lasted is unknown, but perhaps several hundred years. At length, however, as the population rose, the moment of unbearable harassment of the bighorn was reached and the remnants of the once great bands fled from the region.

This probably marked the point of maximum ceremonialism and rock art as the Shoshoneans attempted to ritually bring the vanished game back. When this failed, the tradition of making rock drawings gradually died out. This might have happened some 1,000 years or less ago, about the time the Numic Shoshoneans were abandoning an increasingly harsh environment and starting their treks north and east in search of greener pastures (and more sheep). The disappearance of the sheep and the migration of most of the people brought an end to the ceremonialism recorded on the rocks. At the time of first white contact, the only ritual was a simple round dance held once a year by a few people who had not the slightest knowledge of the meaning of the mysterious rock pictures.

The evidence of the rock drawings suggests that some migrations began at an early date. In southeastern Utah there are sheep with hoofs and men holding weighted atlatls, very like Transitional Period Coso drawings. Men or ideas may have been moving eastward from the Coso region before A.D. 700. By that time the bow was firmly established in the Four Corners as the prime weapon.

Some of the migrating family groups certainly took their sheep-magic tradition with them and used it wherever bighorn and canyon country made ambushing possible.

Occurring with the ubiquitous sheep along the Colorado and San Juan Rivers are patterned-body figures and processions of stick-figures, both late Coso motifs. It is possible that the Shoshonean pattern of sheep-hunting magic travelled to the headwaters of the Colorado and into the Columbia watershed via the Snake River in southern Idaho. An alternate route was along the eastern slope of the Sierra Nevada and through central Oregon. In the gorges of the Columbia, the prehistoric Indians pecked and painted thousands of sheep, often with archers and dogs, both characteristic of the Late Period in the Coso Range.

On the basis of our Coso studies, we believe the drawings there represent some of the earliest rock designs in the country. We also believe that the drawings were made over a period of several thousands of years by the same people, developing their characteristic art forms with little influence from the outside. There is no other area in the western states of comparable size with such a concentration of drawings. Our field count (14,084) covered only the two central canyons, and the outlying sites might easily contain as many more.

In ceremonial rock art, the number of motifs are limited. This is especially noticeable in isolated areas where contact with new and varied ideas is minimal or nonexistent. The same design elements can be repeated with only slight changes for centuries. On the other hand, where there is contact with a higher form of ceremonial or secular art, the adaptation of new forms and ideas can be rapid. Examples of this are the acculturation of the nomadic Navajo to the customs and religious practices of the Pueblo people and the cultural take-over by the nomadic Aztecs of the high culture of the Toltecs.

What is so astonishing about the Coso Range rock art complex is that it apparently developed in almost complete isolation, an island of specialized art tradition. It was surrounded by the Great Basin abstract style from which it sprung, to the north, east and south, and the California polychrome painted styles to the west.

The long span of rock art tradition in the Coso region allows certain conclusions to be drawn bearing on the question of "art for art's sake." Though most of the pictures were primarily made for ritualistic purposes, the steady improvement in technique and detail, especially in the Transitional and Late Periods, demonstrates that the creators took satisfaction in a job ingeniously conceived and well executed. Where one man would crudely abrade a barely recognizable sheep, a few inches long—a job that would take him perhaps a half hour, some of the later artists made highly stylized life-sized sheep, laboriously pecked all over, a job that might take days.

Ceremonial rock art in a primitive society serves two purposes: first, the drawings aid tribal priests or shamans in controlling the forces of nature, increasing the food supply, and in promoting individual and collective well-being; second, the drawings satisfy the innate desire of the creator to make a pleasing image on a rock where nothing had existed before, an image that might carry a part of the artist into the most distant future.

The Coso rock artists did their job well. Through a study of the immense number of drawings they left on the canyon walls—many looking as fresh as if the creator had just put down his basalt chisel—we can reconstruct his hunting methods and attendant rituals. The feathered shamans with ceremonial fringed skirts are there. The shamans wearing sheep horn headdresses are there. The hunters with their atlatls or bows and the long lines of feathered figures are there, pecked into the blue-black basalt. Sheep running, sheep leaping, sheep pursued by dogs, sheep dead, impaled with darts or arrows—all are vividly portrayed on the walls of the long-silent lava gorges.

If our knowledge of the prehistoric inhabitants of the region depended solely on what the archaeologist's shovel and screen turned up, we would have to conclude that their lives were spent in a ceaseless struggle to exist and nothing more—a picture seemingly verified by the culture of the historic Indians of the region.

The great stone galleries of the Coso Range are windows into the past, windows that reveal far more than can be dug from the ground. The rock drawings tell us that for a very long time these ancient people enjoyed a rich ceremonialism connecting the problems of the real world with the powers of the equally real spirit world.

APPENDIX A
METHODS OF RECORDING

The survey of the rock art of the Coso Range involved a number of unique problems. The chief difficulty arose from the fact that the major concentrations of drawings are located in the northern third of the Base, the impact or target area into which test missiles and ordnance of all kinds are fired. This firing is usually discontinued on the weekends so that all our work had to be planned around this schedule. The survey party usually consisted of two cameramen and two recorders: Campbell Grant, James Baird, and Kenneth Pringle, with an extra man recruited from interested friends.

Many of the roads in the survey area are impassible for a standard car and we travelled in two four-wheel-drive vehicles with ample spare water and gas. A base of operations was available near the main sites in a Navy building formerly used by security personnel patrolling the firing range.

The cameramen took many photographs both in color and black-and-white of each section. The recorders, with clip boards and tally sheets listing 33 abstract and 27 naturalistic categories, made as complete a count of the design elements in the main canyons as possible. For the minor surrounding sites, the recording was not so precise. Here photos were taken of all types of elements, and notes were made on the relative abundance of these types.

The engraved rocks, with few exceptions, were fully exposed to the weather and no flash equipment was necessary. An overcast sky was best for picture taking. Bright sunlight, especially if striking the surface at an angle, tends to pick up surface irregularities and obscure details of the design. On the other hand, deeply pecked designs that lack surface contrast can be seen to best advantage with a side light. Many field workers routinely chalk the designs to increase the contrast for photography. This is an extremely poor practice, which distorts the original patterns and destroys the natural contrast, so important in arriving at relative chronology.

The design motif data was later transferred to a master sheet (see sample page 118) and a site record made, giving USGS topo sheet, range, township, section, and elevation, with explicit directions on the easiest way to reach the site.

Weather was a limiting factor in surveying the Coso Range. In the winter, rain and snow can make the rough roads impassible and in the summer, very high temperatures in the basalt gorges makes the work unpleasant and exhausting. Our investigations were carried out from September 1966 through October 1967 with the survey party in the field every other week-end, weather permitting.

1. SITE   Sheep Canyon (S-20)   2. NUMBER   CG Iny-9D   3. COUNTY   Inyo

4. MAP   Coso Peak   5. ELEVATION   4200 – 4300

6. LOCATION   T22S-R40E-S20 1/2 mile below Iny-9C and close to the confluence
of Sheep and Petroglyph Canyons, there are some scattering sites
and an immense site at the lower end of a gorge—drawings on
isolated boulders.

7. DIMENSIONS OF DECORATED AREA   about 1/4 square mile

8. KIND OF ROCK   basalt

9. POSITION OF ROCK   both sides of canyon

10. COLORS

11. DESIGN ELEMENTS   Overwhelmingly realistic—35 abstracts, 841 sheep, 29
dogs, 2 thunderbirds, 8 bowmen—no atlatls. Total 949

12. SUPERIMPOSITION   none

13. EROSION   slight

14. VANDALISM   none

15. ASSOCIATED FEATURES   extensive chipping areas

16. REMARKS   This appears to be the latest major site in the area—most designs
carefully pecked—apparently dogs important at this stage for
driving game.

17. PREVIOUS DESIGNATIONS FOR SITE   none

18. PUBLISHED REFERENCES   none

19. RECORDED BY   Campbell Grant, J. Baird, K. Pringle

20. DATE   9/25/66   21. PHOTOS   color   b&w

APPENDIX B

DISTRIBUTION AND
TALLY OF DESIGN ELEMENTS

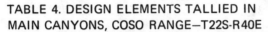

TABLE 4. DESIGN ELEMENTS TALLIED IN
MAIN CANYONS, COSO RANGE—T22S-R40E

Petroglyph Canyon	Iny-7	(P-4)	1047	
	7A	(P-9)	3779	
	7B	(P-8)	30	
	7C	(20)	44	
				4,900
Renegade Canyon	Iny-8	(R-13)	224	
	8A	(R-24)	31	
	8B	(R-25)	2310	
	8C	(R-35)	2004	
	8D	(R-26)	125	
	8E	(R-23)	407	
	8F	(R-8)	1174	
				6,277
Sheep Canyon	Iny-9	(S-10)	167	
	9A	(S-15)	744	
	9B	(S-16)	644	
	9C	(S-17)	224	
	9D	(S-20)	949	
	9E	(S-12)	0 19	
	9F	(S-13)	6	
				2,753
Horse Canyon	Iny-10	(H-8)	154	154
Total				14,084

TABLE 5. Naturalistic Elements, by Site.

Element	Site (INY)																			Totals
	7	7A	7B	7C	8	8A	8B	8C	8D	8E	8F	9	9A	9B	9C	9D	9E	9F	10	
	Naturalistic and stylized elements																			
Anthropomorph:																				
Horned	31	84	8		1	1	21	15			1	1	11	18	2	4			3	201
Paired or in lines	4	12					5	3		1	1	1	3			3			5	33
Patterned body	36	230		2	33	4	125	133	1	1	101		49	13	6	6			5	745
Solid body	22	217			7		72	108	38	1	41	22	73	39	55	14			4	651
With atlatl		4	3				3													10
With bow and arrow	26	92					13	24	2	9	13	7	14	9	2	8			4	223
With other implement		3					7	6					3	1		1				21
Atlatl	5	14	2		1	6	100	157		1	8	5	14	6			2		5	325
Bird	1	14					11	7			2		1							36
Clouds and rain	4	1					3	4					1	2						15
Deer	5	57	1	5	3		15	15	2	2	7									112
Dog	4	71			1		22	18		6	7	15	37	8	2	29	1		4	225
Hand or foot		7			1		5						1			1				15
Lizard	2	23					11	6			1		7	1		1				52
Medicine bag	2	71			2		24	22	1		27	5	15	12	2	2				185
Projectile foreshafts	2						5	1				5	3							16
Sheep:																				
Boat-shaped (horns front)	62	260					92	91			5		50	116	15	18				704
Double-ended	2	22					7	15					1	2	3	2				54
Heads only	18	75			4		190	56			9		11	18	7					388
Horns front	5	238			3		144	229	20	201	311	31	94	22	7	31	4		12	1352
Horns side	396	1338	11	19	34	5	489	407	25	160	240	33	137	226	142	786	5	6	42	4501
Impaled	6	31					8	16	1	6	14		12	5	4	2				105
Rectangular		6					1	2			2					2				13
With embryo		3					1				1		1							6
With interior design	10	30					9	7					5	3	2	1				68
Snake	7	45			3		18	30	4	2	24	3	6	9		3	1			151
Tracks—bear, deer, sheep, misc. (not individual tracks—but occurences)	1	10			4		9	9			2									40
Totals	652	2958	25	26	97	16	1410	1393	96	398	811	128	552	512	201	914	13	6	80	10288

120

TABLE 5. (Contd.) Abstract Elements, by Site.

Element	7	7A	7B	7C	8	8A	8B	8C	8D	8E	8F	9	9A	9B	9C	9D	9E	9F	10	Totals
										Abstract elements										
Checkerboard					1		5	8			1									16
Circle:																				
Bisected	13	17			1		3	5			3		1	2					2	47
Bisected with line	13	15		1			3	2			3	1	3						4	45
Cluster	7	20					35	30	1		5	3	5	5		1				113
Concentric	8	37			2		32	15			5	2	5	4					4	114
Concentric and spoked	9	13		1	1		20	10			1			1						55
Connected with line	10	34			1	1	19	21	1		4		4	10	1				20	102
Outlined	5	52	5				32	45	1		5		10	7	1		3		1	181
Rayed	13	9			2		19	21			8	3	5	4		5			2	88
Solid		18					4	4			3	2	3						1	37
Spoked	4	20			4		21				2		2						1	59
Cross	3	11			9	3	12	3		2	5	3	3	3					1	48
Curvilinear meander	11	38		2			29	37	2	2	6		11	20	5		1		5	166
Dot patterns	13	35		1	2		33	33					8	13	1				2	149
Dots connected	6	6			10		5	5				2		6	1	1				44
Grid:																				
Oval	4	19			3		21	18			18		6	1	1				5	95
Square	4	10			3		47	15			18		6							104
Ladder:																				
Double riser		9			4		6	7	5			1	2							34
Single riser	3	9				6	10	13	1		1		4						1	41
Lines:																				
Parallel	6	11			4		23	7	1		1	1	3	2						60
Wavy	8	26		2			29	16	1		1		12	2					3	100
Zigzag	11	4					3	2												20
Miscellaneous:																				
Curvilinear		37			5		58	38		3	24	15	17	2					10	214
Rectilinear	3	32			1		24	35			34	6	14	4		2			3	158
Pit-and-groove	1	2					18													21
Rainbow	3	5			4			2		3				1						18
Rake	6	15			2		33	22			3		6	6	1				3	99
Rectilinear neander	3	12					2				2			2	1					23
Shield:																				
Rectilinear	125	113		11	35	1	185	97	4	3	136		26	11	7	12	1		2	765
Round or oval	101	182			30	4	149	81	14	3	56	6	32	26	6	13	1		4	708
Spiral	1	4			3		9	5	1		3		1			1				27
Star	1	5					11	3					1						1	21
Triangle		2						3			12		4							21
Totals	395	821	5	18	127	15	910	612	33	9	363	39	192	132	23	35	6		74	3796

APPENDIX C

CONTACT WITH OTHER AREAS IN THE WEST SHOWN BY DESIGN ELEMENTS

The roots of the Coso rock art lie in the Great Basin Abstract tradition, but the highly individual and characteristic designs that mark the Late Period developed in almost complete isolation from outside influences.

There are a few scattered examples (not more than 12) in the Petroglyph Canyon drainage of design elements that are well known in other parts of the country, particularly in the Southwest.

The highly stylized drawing in figure b below from Petroglyph Canyon strongly resembles the adjoining female figure from a Basketmaker site in northern Arizona. Both show exaggerated sexual parts and head appendages resembling the Hopi girl's hairdressing.

The thunderbird, (see figure below), from Petroglyph Canyon and two others in lower Sheep Canyon are the only examples in the area. They are basically similar to the stylized thunderbird so common in most of North America but rare in the Great Basin and nonexistent in California west of the Sierra Nevada.

Another design element wide-spread through western America, especially in the Great Plains and Southwest, is the bear track. It has many minor variations but is recognizable

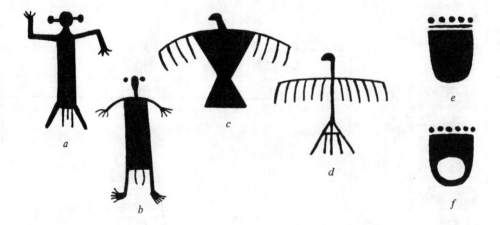

Intrusive Design Elements Found in the Coso Range. a. Female with side-lock hair dressing, northwestern Arizona (after Kidder and Guernsey, 1919). b. Petroglyph Canyon (P-9). c. Thunderbird, Cieneguilla, near Santa Fe, New Mexico. d. Petroglyph Canyon (P-4). e. Bear track, Indian Creek, southeastern Utah. f. Petroglyph Canyon (P-4).

wherever it occurs. The example from Petroglyph Canyon (see figure *f* on opposite page) is one of several groups in the region.

Judging from the patination on these three intrusive design motifs, they are of the Transitional Period.

A number of typical Coso design elements occur in different parts of the western states reflecting migrations of people from the area as well as diffusion of ideas from the focus of intense preoccupation with sheep hunting in the Coso Range.

The most prominant motif, of course, is the bighorn sheep, and this is fully discussed in Appendix E.

The patterned-body anthropomorph, so typical of the Transitional and Late Periods in the Coso, occurs frequently in the Colorado drainage, particularly in northern Arizona

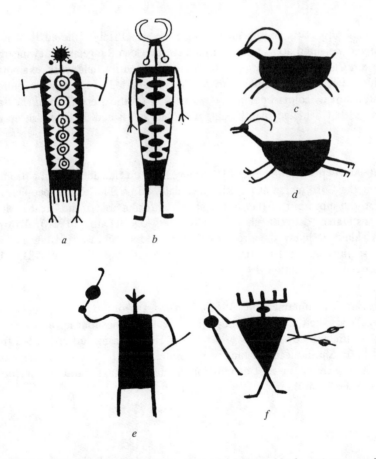

Coso Range Design Elements Found in the Southwest. a. Patterned-body anthropomorph, Renegade Canyon (R-25). b. Near Winslow, Arizona. c. Bighorn sheep, Sheep Canyon (S-20). d. Monument Valley, Utah. e. Anthropomorph with atlatl, Petroglyph Canyon (P-8). f. San Juan River, southeastern Utah.

and southern Utah. Note the great similarity between examples *a* and *b* of the figure on page 123. One is from Renegade Canyon; the other, from near Winslow, Arizona.

Southern Nevada was a contact area between the desert Shoshoneans and the early Anasazi people developing from Basketmakers into a pottery and pueblo dwelling culture. The most westerly Anasazi villages were along the Virgin and Muddy Rivers, near the Colorado River. In the Valley of Fire State Park near Overton, several Type 3 atlatls (without weights) occur on the red sandstone with sheep and two Coso "medicine bags." Other elements are the usual Great Basin Abstract and the square- and triangular-bodied figures so typical of Southwest Basketmaker and early Pueblo. In the extreme southern tip of Nevada, in Grapevine Canyon State Park, there are sheep and several Type 3 atlatls. In the Valley of Fire and at Grapevine Canyon, there are single examples of the true "shield" figure so characteristic of the Southwest and of the Great Plains. These two isolated examples mark a far western extension of this motif that reached its peak in the Fremont region of eastern Utah.

Until this manuscript was approaching completion, we firmly believed that aboriginal drawings of the weighted atlatl were confined to the Coso Range and a few nearby areas in southeastern California. This was on the basis of extensive field work, examination of photographic collections and printed surveys. Within a period of weeks, we acquired from two separate sources, color slides from two sites in southeastern Utah in the San Juan River drainage that depicted men holding weighted atlatls and darts and sheep impaled with darts.

The atlatl drawings from southeastern Utah may indicate that ideas, if not people, were coming from the Coso region at a fairly early date. Some Shoshonean people may well have been on the move out of the southeastern California area of the Great Basin earlier than the postulated date of about 1,000 years ago (Lamb, 1958). Wormington (1955:188) thinks it likely the Fremont Culture people of eastern Utah and western Colorado were Shoshonean. They first appear in the Southwest soon after A.D. 600 (Noel Morss, personal communication, 1967).

Steward (personal communication, 1968) bears out Wormington's speculation with another speculation: he thinks that it might have been the Shoshonean Hopi who brought an Anasazi culture into Utah. How or when the Hopi became differentiated from the other Great Basin Shoshonean-speaking people is unknown. It does appear, however, that the Shoshoneans were at the root of most of the major petroglyph developments in the Southwest and the Great Basin.

APPENDIX D
THE DESERT BIGHORN

The bighorn or mountain sheep occurs in western North America from the Brooks Range in Alaska to southern Baja California in Mexico. There are two species: the Rocky Mountain bighorn (*Ovis canadensis*) occupying the southern region from southeastern British Columbia to northern Mexico, which varies in color from dark gray-brown to the pale buff of the Desert bighorn; and the northern bighorn (*Ovis dalli*), found in Alaska, the Yukon and Central British Columbia, which is somewhat smaller than the Rocky Mountain sheep and has more slender horns. They vary in color from white for Dall sheep to brown-black for Stone sheep.

The earliest description is found in a report written by Francisco Vasquez Coronado from Cibola (New Mexico) to Viceroy Mendoza in 1540:

> They have many animals—Bears, Tigers, Lions, Porcupines and some Sheep as big as a Horse, with very large horns and little tails. I have seen some of these horns, the size of which is something to marvel at.

Bighorn Sheep Ram of Southern Nevada. (Photo by Charles G. Hansen, Bureau of Sport Fisheries and Wildlife, Nevada.)

Over 200 years later in 1776, the Spanish explorer Father Silvestre de Escalante crossed the Colorado near the present Utah-Arizona border and noted:

> Through here wild sheep live in such abundance that their tracks
> are like those of great flocks of domestic sheep. They are larger
> than the domestic breed of the same form, but much swifter.

There is no more sought-after trophy in the world of sport than the heavy curving horns of a bighorn ram and the incessant hunting of this magnificent game animal has sharply reduced their numbers, especially in the United States and Mexico. They are strictly protected in both countries today, but poaching continues in many areas.

In 1922, Ernest Thompson Seton estimated the bighorn in the United States as follows:

Arizona	3,500
California	3,500
Colorado	8,000
Idaho	1,500
Montana (including Glacier Park)	5,000
Nevada	500
New Mexico	500
Texas	500
Utah	1,000
Wyoming (including Yellowstone Park)	4,000
Total	28,000

Recent estimates based on Department of Fish and Game surveys give a California population of about 2,500. Similar surveys carried out in Nevada and Arizona estimate their Desert bighorn populations in Nevada at 2,500, and Arizona at 3,500. These surveys, using every modern technique such as the use of the helicopter, are undoubtedly more accurate than methods used in arriving at Seton's figures. The Fish and Game authorities in Nevada, Arizona, and New Mexico are confident that the Desert bighorn is more than holding its own and allow a small number of mature rams to be harvested by hunters every year.

The preferred habitat of the bighorn is in the roughest mountain ranges; but, undoubtedly, before the coming of the white man with his deadly rifle the sheep utilized the foothills and plains far more than they do today for spring and early summer foraging. Their food is chiefly grass in the northern ranges and primarily browse in the southern or desert ranges.

The sheep hunted by the prehistoric Indians of southeastern California was the Desert bighorn or Nelson bighorn (*Ovis canadensis nelsoni*). These sheep occupy the arid ranges rimming the desert plains of the Southwest and the Great Basin. It is a land of rocky crags, cinder cones, barren mesas and little water, but the Desert bighorn is perfectly adopted for life in such an environment.

There are still some bands of sheep in Inyo County that appear to be surviving well in spite of some illegal hunting. Recent estimates place their numbers at about 1,000. These bands inhabit the southern Sierra Nevada, the Inyo Range, the mountains surrounding Death Valley, and the Argus Range that borders the Coso region on the east. (The Sierra bands are not Desert bighorn, but a closely related type of *Ovis canadensis.*)

The bighorn of the Coso Range, so dramatically preserved on stone by the ancient hunters, became extinct in the region many years ago, perhaps long before the coming of the white man. There is recent evidence, however, that a number still exist in the adjacent Argus Range. According to John Parrish of the California Fish and Game, tracks have been seen near the summit of Maturango Peak and at Tennessee Springs in the last 10 years. Sheep were seen in Mountain Springs Canyon in 1965 and five bighorn were recorded north of Wilson Canyon.

About 20 years ago, a dead bighorn sheep was found in the Haiwee Canal above Haiwee Dam, raising the possibility that it had come from the Coso Range. As it is generally conceded that the Sierra bighorn bands do not cross the Owens Valley into the desert ranges, and the Desert bighorn do not migrate into the Sierra Nevada, this piece of evidence is difficult to explain, but until actual sightings or tracks have been reported from the Coso Range, they must be considered extinct there.

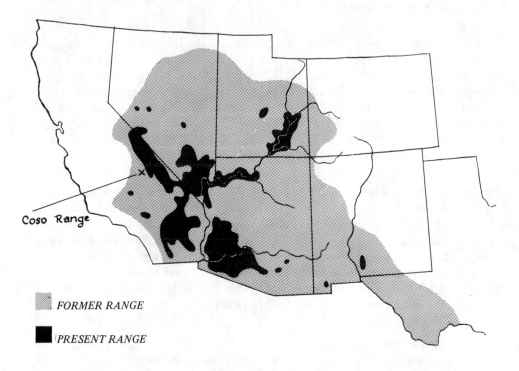

Coso Range

FORMER RANGE

PRESENT RANGE

Comparison of Former and Present Ranges of the Desert Bighorn. Information supplied by Ralph and Florence Welles, Nevada Fish and Game Commission, New Mexico Department of Game and Fish, Arizona Game and Fish Department, and Utah Department of Fish and Game.

It is possible to reconstruct the life and habits of the sheep of the region through a remarkable book, *The Bighorn of Death Valley*. This book is the first complete survey on the Desert bighorn, and the authors, Ralph and Florence Welles, devoted years to the closest study of the Death Valley bighorn bands. Most of the following has been drawn from this source.

The Desert bighorn sheep differ basically from domestic sheep in lacking true fleece; their coats are quite similar to those of deer. The Desert bighorn is a smaller animal than its close relation, the Rocky Mountain bighorn (*Ovis canadensis*). Of 44 rams measured in Arizona and Nevada (Aldous, et al. 1958 and Russo, 1956) the average was 162 pounds and the maximum was 200. The average of 20 ewes was 105 pounds with a maximum of 126. By contrast, Seton (1929) records a ram from the northern Rockies that weighed 316 pounds and stated that the average for the bigger Rocky Mountain rams would be about 300 pounds. Bighorn rams develop immense curving horns (one record set from British Columbia weighs over 40 pounds). The ewes have short, slender, curved spike horns.

The bighorn are poor runners on the level and when pursued, take refuge in high rocky country where their climbing ability is spectacular. They are able to climb or descend almost vertical rock faces at top speed due to the curious formation of their hoofs. The concave hoof pads are tough and rubber-like with shock absorbent qualities enabling them to grip the rock surfaces.

Their food is mainly browse in the desert ranges: annual plants in the spring and summer, and many varieties of shrubs throughout the year. Some of the desert plants eaten by sheep are Galleta grass (*Hilaria rigida*), Mormon tea (*Ephedra sp.*), Honey mesquite (*Prosopis chilensis*), Rush bebbia (*Bebbia juncea*), Buckwheat (*Eriogonum sp.*), willow (*Salix sp.*), Mountain mahogany (*Cercocarpus ledifolius*), and lupines (*Lupinus sp.*). If food is scarce, the bighorn will eat practically any plant in the range. The sheep move rapidly as they feed, nipping a bite here and there. This habit insures the survival of many plants that would be destroyed by close cropping.

Bighorn bands vary in size with the scarcity or abundance of food and water. In the Death Valley region where both items are perpetually scarce, the observed bands varied from 3 to 37 with an average of 9. Normally the Desert bighorn lives out its life in a restricted home range, seldom travelling beyond a 20-mile radius of the home water supply. Abundant rains, however, insuring a good supply of temporary water in rock basins or streams, allow the bands to move more freely and to exploit new feeding grounds. During hot weather, the sheep drink every 3 to 5 days, but when the weather turns cold, the animals usually drink every 10 to 14 days.

The bands spend their days in alternate periods of eating and resting with considerable time spent in playing and frisking about, particularly among the younger members of the band. The rams only travel with the ewes and lambs during the rutting season. In Death Valley this period starts in late June and lasts til mid-December with the peak of activity from August through September. At all times the leader of the band is a ewe.

The most spectacular activity of the bighorn is the ritualistic duel or butting contest between mature rams during the mating season. This is in no sense a fight to the death between rams fighting over ewes, and the greatest damage is usually no more than an occasional broken horn. It seems motivated by a powerful urge triggered by the mating instinct.

There seem to be certain rules and routines followed in these butting matches. The engagement may commence with the two rams standing side by side, but facing in opposite directions. Grunting and blowing, they strike at each other's testicles with their sharp hoofs. After several minutes of this preliminary, they walk away from one another until they are from 20 to 40 feet apart. Simultaneously they turn, rear and charge forward on stiffened hind legs. As the two heads crash together, the crack of the heavy horns can be heard for great distances. Dazed, the rams back away, and a few minutes later, go at it again. This may go on for a considerable time at the peak of the mating season, and at the end, both contestants often walk away side by side.

The height of the lambing season varies with the climate, but is usually around March. One lamb is normally dropped; twins are rare. The mortality among lambs in the Death Valley region is very high (estimated by the Welles' to be as high as 90%). Accidental falls from cliffs accounts for some of this; disease and nutritional deficiencies may also be factors; but little is known to account for such a high first year mortality rate. If the sheep lives through this first critical year, its chances to reach an age of over 10 years are good.

There is little doubt that diseases of domestic sheep have taken a heavy toll among the bighorn and that competition for forage with domestic stock and wild burros, especially near water supplies, has probably been a factor in the decline of the Desert bighorn. The natural enemies of the bighorn are few; mountain lions, bobcats, and eagles doubtless take a few lambs every year, but man is the chief menace. His incessant diversion of vital water supplies and continued illegal hunting are a constant threat to the remaining bands.

Ralph and Florence Welles, who have studied the problem more intensely than anyone, put it this way:

> The future of the bighorn is inexorably tied to the attitude of man toward the natural world in which he lives. The nature of this attitude may determine the quality as well as the quantity of the encroachment with which the entire world community will have to contend—whether as Aldo Leopold expressed it, man continues to consider himself the conqueror of the living world or attains the wisdom to become a fellow citizen in it, sharing with other creatures the rights and privileges of living.

APPENDIX E

THE BIGHORN SHEEP IN NORTH AMERICAN ROCK ART

There is no rock drawing motif that occurs more frequently in the western United States than the bighorn sheep. The original range (see map page 127) was immense, but the drawings of the animal are mainly concentrated in a few areas. Most of the drawings are done in a realistic manner, but in the Coso Range and in the Four Corners region (where Arizona, New Mexico, Utah and Colorado join) there is much stylization.

The sheep is rarely drawn with horns to the front except in the Coso region. A common type throughout the Great Basin and in the Four Corners area of the Southwest is what can be described as the "fat-tailed" sheep (see figure below). This type is completely lacking in the Coso Range. In southern Utah and northern Arizona, the sheep drawings often show a characteristic rare elsewhere—the hoofs of the animal are represented by a single or double forward projection.

At the principal concentrations, certain factors are invariably present. The first requisite is, of course, ample patinated rock surfaces; these are usually of basalt, but along the Colorado and its tributaries the rock is predominately sandstone, which can build up a very dark patina and is infinitely easier to engrave than basalt. These sites are in canyon country where deep gorges and rough terrain afford conditions for communal sheep hunting and driving past ambushes. John Muir (1901) noted an abundance of rock-piled hunting blinds in Nevada similar to those in the Coso Range, and doubtless the same type of blinds could be located in all areas where the bighorn drawings are concentrated.

a

b

a. "Fat-tailed" Sheep, Northern Arizona. b. Another characteristic sheep from northeastern Arizona with hoof indication. (Both after Kidder and Guernsey, 1919.)

The indication of sheep by drawing the horns alone appears to be limited to the Great Basin in southeastern California and adjacent areas in Nevada, and can be presumed to have diffused from the Coso region. The sheep pictures are overwhelmingly of the pecked or abraded type, but there are isolated examples in some areas, usually on sandstone or granite, of painted sheep. Where these are found in caves, they are in a fair state of preservation, but examples on cliffs or exposed boulders are badly eroded. The one painted example in the Coso Range, modeled on the Late Period pecked style, is in the last stages of obliteration.

The most interesting sheep paintings are found in remote canyons of the Sierra de San Francisco in central Baja California. They are often life-sized and done quite realistically. Other examples occur in western Wyoming rock shelters and in western Texas.

The map on page 132 locates a number of sites where bighorn sheep are pictured. While very far from being a complete record, there are enough that have been recorded to give us an interesting pattern. With the exception of the sites along the Columbia (mainly under water today) the principal concentrations are all in the territory of the Shoshoneans. Each dot represents a site in all instances except the Coso-Death Valley area and the Four Corners. In these regions there were far too many sites to indicate on a map of this scale, the Coso Range alone having more than 60 sites.

The Shoshonean migrations from southeastern California described by Heizer and Baumhoff (1962:14-15) fanning out north and east, almost certainly carried the sheep hunting magic tradition with them.

These migrations brought new ideas to the rock art of the Columbia-Fraser Plateau and the Southwest. The association of sheep, bowmen and highly decorative anthropomorphs so characteristic of the Coso Range, is found in southeastern Utah, in northern Arizona, and along the middle Columbia. There are different conceptions of these elements in each area, but the possibility of a common origin in southeastern California cannot be discounted. The concentrations in the Columbia River region and in the Four Corners suggest a sheep cult similar to the one we have postulated for the Coso area. Well-carved stone figurines with sheep heads from the Columbia might have played a part in the cult ritual.

The evidence of the rock drawings indicates that the sheep-hunting magic idea arrived late in the Columbia region. There are no atlatls pictured there, only bowmen, and at a number of sites along the middle Columbia, sheep with horns to the front are fairly common. This convention is the most marked characteristic of the Transitional and Late Coso Period. With the exception of one example in Nevada, all the known horns-to-the-front sheep are concentrated in the Coso Range and along the Columbia. It can be argued that the examples from the Columbia represent independent invention, but we believe they indicate diffusion.

The major migration routes, based on the occurrences of bighorn sheep in the rock drawings, lay north along the eastern flank of the Sierra Nevada and east following the Colorado and its tributaries. The sheep site map shows the route east skirting the Grand

Canyon by way of southern Utah. Either route would eventually have brought them in contact with the Salish in the Columbia drainage. The concentration of sheep sites in the basaltic rocks of southern Oregon, recently recorded by Malcolm Loring, represents a point where the sheep and rocks suitable for pecking coincided. The map below shows their isolation between the Columbia River and Coso-Death Valley concentrations. South of these Oregon sites there is a long blank area until the California-Nevada line swings to

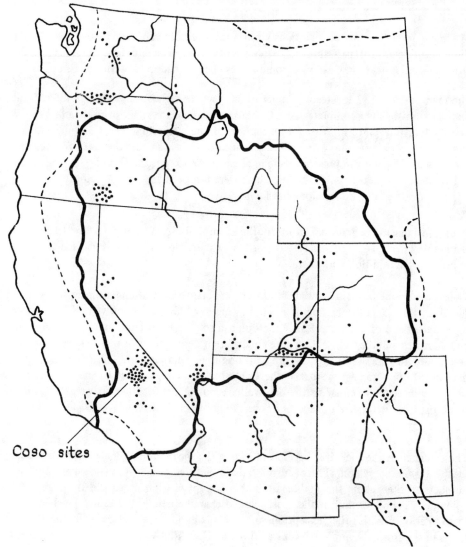

Coso sites

———— Shoshonean Territory at Time of First White Contact (Stewart, 1966; Kroeber, 1925)

– – – – – – Former Range of Bighorn Sheep (Hall, 1959)

Bighorn Sheep Drawing Sites. Density only approximate; a dot can represent 1 sheep or 1,000 sheep according to size of site

the southeast. This region is high, flat desert with few appropriate rocks. Between the Oregon concentration and the Columbia River to the north, light-colored rocks are dominant and most of the sheep sites are painted.

There are a few sites featuring bighorn sheep that do not fit the pattern that we have proposed. Near the town of Moapa in southeastern Nevada, there is a site where many recent-appearing drawings are pecked into patinated rhyolite. These feature sheep, dogs, and horsemen wearing hats. They are pecked over older abstract drawings. There seems to be no doubt that they are of Indian origin, but the close juxtaposition of the white men and the bighorn is puzzling and would seem to rule out hunting magic unless we consider the possibility that the horsemen in this instance were considered "fair game" along with the sheep!

The sheep drawings from southern New Mexico and western Texas are mainly square-bodied with interior designs and show both Pueblo and Great Plains influence. These are probably the work of the Apache. There are two sites—one at Three Rivers in New Mexico, and the other in nearby western Texas—that depict the horns of the sheep realistically with thickness and correct curl. This is unique in western sheep drawing where the usual method is to indicate the heavy horns with simple curved lines. Representations of sheep and atlatls occur together at one site near El Paso. In central Oregon, Idaho, Wyoming and Montana, where dark, patinated rocks are lacking, there are a few painted sites, mainly finger-painted in the crudest manner.

It seems evident that through the Shoshonean migrations from the Death Valley-Coso region, pictorial ideas connected with sheep hunting and attendant ritual became widely disseminated in the Western states.

APPENDIX F
MATERIAL CULTURE ITEMS
SHOWN IN ROCK DRAWINGS

WEAPONS

    Atlatls
    Darts
    Bow and arrows
    Spear and arrow point foreshafts

CEREMONIAL COSTUME AND PARAPHERNALIA

    Headdresses
        Horned
            Short spikes
            Bighorns
        Feathered
            Single feather
            Double feather
            Many feathered

    Earrings

    Fringed skirts

    Body paint

    Medicine bags

    Unknown ceremonial objects

APPENDIX G
GEOLOGY OF THE
COSO ROCK ART REGION
by J. Kenneth Pringle

The rock pictures are found inscribed on basaltic rocks of early Pleistocene age. Some of the basalts contain a high enough percentage of olivine phenocrysts (as high as 25% in some cases) so that they can be called olivine-basalts. Both olivine-basalts and normal basalts were used for rock drawings, as their exposed surfaces weather to a very dark shiny lustre. This contrasts with the lighter unexposed interior. Most of the area under examination is covered by flows of these two types of basalt. There are, in addition, a few flows with a slightly different composition. These often tend to deteriorate rapidly, and many of the designs pecked on such basalts are barely visible today.

Geologically, these basalts reflect the tectonics of both the local region and the general physiographic province to which they belong. The area is situated in the extreme southwest corner of the Basin-Range Province. This province is characterized by North-South trending ranges with intervening valleys that have internal drainage. It extends from the Sierra to the Rocky Mountains in Utah. The Coso and Argus Ranges bordering and containing the basalt flows are good examples of this Basin-Range province physiography.

Locally, the tectonic situation is quite complex. The basalts we see on the surface are a result of a multitude of fractures which criss-cross the region. These fractures provided the conduits for a deep-seated magma to come to the surface as flows and, where adequate pressure was available, to be expressed as cinder cones, pressure ridges, etc. In one part of the area, that of Coso Hot Springs, the magma was forcibly intruded causing a doming and fracturing of the surface. The basalts then poured out leaving a large empty space. When the space became too great to sustain the overlying material, a collapse took place and a subsidence structure was the result. The basalts immediately to the east of Coso Hot Springs have a step-faulted appearance as viewed from the Springs, but when viewed on aerial photographs the major faults are seen to be arc-like in structure with minor faults radiating out from a focal point in the area of the Springs. Areas of subsidence can be found by tracing the faulting pattern on topographic maps. In all, three of these collapse areas are evident.

The topography was further changed by renewed volcanic activity along the radial fractures. Water then cut deep, steep-sided canyons along the arc-like fractures, following for a way, then encountering points of weakness at radial fractures, crossing over to the next lower arc-like fracture and continuing on to emerge into either the Coso Hot Springs Basin or another basin farther to the south called Airport Lake Basin. Any given canyon will usually start out being very shallow and rapidly become deep only to cross one of the steps and almost disappear as a canyon. This was advantageous to the Indians because of the ease of access into the canyons afforded, and it is at these points that the greatest concentration of pecked designs occur.

In other parts of the area under examination the basalts have formed high plateau structures. For a few feet below the rim of the mesas the basalts are exposed with vertical sides. Below this it is primarily composed of blocky detritus. In some places, either due to faulting or slumpage, natural passes are made onto the tops of the flows, and immediately around these crossing points numerous rock drawings are found. On top of the flows are spots where the basalt has domed up. These are also inscribed.

One remaining type of basaltic structure was used by the ancient artists. Near Silver and Coso Peaks there are many pressure ridges of basalt. This area is high enough to be in the Piñon belt occupied by the Indians every fall. Almost every smooth dark outcrop of this type has a sampling of designs.

APPENDIX H
ADJACENT OCCUPATION SITES
by James W. Baird

In the course of the petroglyph survey and from information provided by local inhabitants, twenty-four rock shelters have been located in the Coso and Argus Mountains within the Naval Weapons Center boundaries. These rock shelters all show evidence of occupation by early man. In addition to the rock shelters, numerous house rings, chipping sites, hunting blinds and camp sites have been located.

To date, only two rock shelters have been excavated: the Ray Cave (Iny-349) and the Chapman Cave, both named after the local youths who discovered and reported them.

Since examination of the artifact materials have not been completed, the following summary should be viewed as a preliminary statement on the contents of these two sites.

Both sites were in geologically similar settings: located about 15 feet below the rim of pleistocene basalt flows where the flows were in conjunction with the talus slope; both measured about 12 by 15 feet with a maximum ceiling height of 3 1/2 to 4 feet; and both terminated in hard consolidated rock at a depth of about 6 feet.

The Ray Cave site is located on a canyon rim 3/4 of a mile southeast of Renegade Canyon. Just below the site at 5,000 feet the small canyon drops sharply in a series of dry falls before emptying into the China Lake basin at approximately 2,000 feet elevation.

Cursory examination of the exposed side walls indicates that it is a homogeneous deposit containing rock fall, small lenses of water-laid silt, and a few ash lenses interspersed as remnants of hearth fires, all in a matrix composed mostly of wind blown silt.

An ash lens from the 32-inch level in the center of the shelter gave a carbon 14 date of 1500 years bp ± 95 years. A similar ash lens under a large boulder at the 48- to 52-inch level has yet to be dated. Two carrying baskets, a pitched water olla, and a seed beater, all in good condition, were found by the original discoverers. With the baskets were several tin cans, one of which was subsequently sent to the Continental Can Company, where it was identified as a type being manufactured between 1885 and 1900.

Artifacts recovered mainly consisted of unshaped unifaced and bifaced milling stones, manos, projectile points, flake and core scrapers, hammerstones, shell and bone beads, a chuckawalla hook, awls and many unclassifiable fragments of artifacts. The types of points that have been found include: Desert side notched, Cottonwood triangular, Elko

Eared, and Pinto points. Chipping waste (mostly obsidian) decreases from top to bottom of the deposit although the size of the individual flakes increases from top to bottom.

The Chapman site is located 2 miles east of Louisiana Butte in the upper end of Renegade Canyon. The cave is just below the rim of a large basalt flow which separates Renegade Canyon from Louisiana Butte, at an elevation of 5,800 feet.

The cave was filled with a homogeneous, windblown deposit, without any natural stratification. There were from 1 to 2 feet of rat nest overburden in the back of the shelter.

The Chapman site was chosen for excavation because of a bundle of cut arrow shafts (carrizo grass) that was found on the surface. Some of the shafts were decorated with black spirals. A number of hardwood foreshafts occurred in association with carrizo grass shafts.

Five cache pits were excavated. They varied in depth from the surface to 4 feet. All were lined with large basketry fragments. One flexed burial was found in association with one of the cache pits. There were a total of two flexed burials, one partial cremation and scattered parts of individuals.

Two small unfired clay vessels, about 1 1/2 inches high, two effigy figures, about 4 inches high, and many fragments of desert brown ware were recovered in the first 14 inches of deposit in the forward half of the rock shelter. This is in contrast with the Ray site which had no clay or pottery fragments. Atlatl points occurred in the lower levels indicating possible long occupancy of the site. One small basket in good condition was located about a foot from the surface.

Artifacts recovered were similar to those found in the Ray Cave mainly consisting of milling stones, manos, projectile points, flake and core scrapers, hammerstones, shell beads, awls, pottery fragments, and again many unclassifiable fragments of artifacts.

APPENDIX I

AUTHOR'S UPDATE
TO THE 6th PRINTING

In many rock shelters in South Africa, there are Bushman paintings of men and game animals. The animal most often featured is the magestic eland, largest of the antelopes and weighing up to 1200 pounds. The Bushmen regularly hunt this huge animal for its abundant fatty meat.

It is tempting to apply the hunting magic theory here but the resemblances between the bighorn hunters and the eland hunters are superficial. Where the bighorn sheep is a wary animal and difficult to hunt, the eland with its great bulk is an easy prey. It can be run down by men on foot or driven close to the hunter's camp before being killed.

Bushmen interviewed in this century and in the nineteenth century were unanimous in their belief that the eland was a supernatural deity and a center of their religious practices. According to Leslie-Williams (1983:49-54) it is the symbolic function of the animal rather than its food value that explains the prominence of the eland in Bushman rock paintings. The ethnological records make no mention of hunting magic.

In the Kalahari Desert region, hunters perform an "eland potency dance" near the carcass of a freshly killed eland. The hunters believe that the potency of the eland can be transferred to the shamans, thus increasing their power during trances. The rock paintings often depict medicine men in association with dead or dying eland.

Perhaps the Coso bighorn hunters drew power from the dead sheep, obviously their most revered animal. Unfortunately, we have no ethnological informants to explain the thousands of petroglyphs of the bighorn sheep. There are many Coso petroglyphs that could suggest a possible power relationship between man and bighorn. There are abundant scenes of sheep together with armed hunters or with humans wearing headdresses and with decorated bodies. In many instances sheep are superimposed over decorated humans (possible shamans). See pages 35, 57, 64, 68, 69.

Since the first printing of this book, there have been several new theories on the formation of patina or desert varnish that question the Flamand and Willcox studies. The first theory holds that patina is formed by external and biological forces. Using electronic microscopy and energy dispersive x-ray analyses, investigators have postulated that the desert varnish is created by wind and waterborn manganese-concentrating micro-organisms deposited on the rock surface (Dorn and Oberlander 1981:1245-1247).

In 1983 two Caltech scientists came up with another theory. For their study they used infrared spectroscopy, a technique which illuminates mineral samples with infrared light and records the pattern of absorbed wavelengths. The samples which included basalt, granite, quartzite, sandstone, feldspar and rhyolite, revealed that clay (70%) was the principal constituent in desert varnish with 30% oxides of iron and manganese.

The investigators concluded that most of the patina derives from sources outside the rock rather than from oxides leached out of the rock. Fine wind-blown particles of clay carry small amounts of iron and manganese oxides. The dry, fluffy clay particles depend on the oxides to form a resistant cementing agent, and the oxides require the clay particles for transportation and deposition. When moisture forms on the rock surface, it creates a thin film of clay and when the water evaporates, tiny amounts of iron and manganese are deposited on the surface (Rossman and Potter 1983).

Most of the studies agree that the darkening of the rock or patina is caused by iron and manganese oxides, but the mechanics of the process differ.

DORN, R. I. and T. M. OBERLANDER. *Microbial Origin of Desert Varnish. Science* 213 (11) 1245-1247, 1981.
ROSSMAN, GEORGE R. and RUSSEL M. POTTER. *Origin of Desert Varnish. The Artifact,* 18 (1-2). San Luis Obispo County Archaeological Society. 1983.
LEWIS-WILLIAMS, J. DAVID. *The Rock Art of Southern Africa.* Cambridge University Press. 1983.

BIBLIOGRAPHY

ALDOUS, M. CLAIR. "Trapping and Tagging of Bighorn Sheep," in Second Bighorn Council Transactions, 1958, pp. 36–39.

ALDOUS, M. CLAIR, FRANK C. CRAIGHEAD, JR., and GEORGE A. DEVAN. "Some Weights and Measurements of Desert Bighorn Sheep," *Journal of Wildlife Management,* Vol. 22 (1958) pp. 444–45.

ALLEN, J. C. "Ecology and Management of Nelson's Bighorn in the Nevada Mountain Ranges," in Transactions of the North American Wildlife Conference, Vol. 4, 1939, pp. 253–56.

ANONYMOUS. "Picture Writing in Pictograph Canyon" (Report of an Explorer Scout trip to Renegade Canyon), *Southwest Museum Masterkey* (Los Angeles), Vol 13, No. 3 (1939) pp. 105–06.

ANTEVS, E. *The Great Basin* Part III. *Climatic Changes and Pre-White Man.* University of Utah Bulletin, Vol. 38, No. 20, 1948. pp. 168–91.

——. "Geologic-Climatic Dating in the West,'" *American Antiquity,* Vol. 20 (1055), pp. 317-35.

BAEGERT, JACOB. "An Account of the Aboriginal Inhabitants of the California Peninsula," Annual Report of the Smithsonian Institution, Washington, D.C., 1872, pp. 360–61.

BESCHEL, RONALD E. "Dating Rock Surfaces by Lichen Growth and Its Application to Glaciology and Physiography (Lichenometry)," in *Geology of the Arctic,* Vol. II, G. O. University of Toronto Press, 1961.

BLANC, ROBERT P., and GEORGE B. CLEVELAND. "Pleistocene Lakes of Southeastern California, Part 1," Mineral Information Service, California State Division of Mines and Geology (San Francisco), Vol. 14, No. 4 (1961), pp. 1–8.

BOLTON, HERBERT E. *Pageant in the Wilderness. The Story of the Escalante Expedition to the Interior Basin.* Utah State Historical Society, 1950. P. 228.

CAIN, H. T. *Petroglyphs of Central Washington.* Seattle, University of Washington Press, 1950.

COSGROVE, C. B. *Caves of the Upper Gila and Hueco Areas in New Mexico and Texas.* Papers of the Peabody Museum, Vol. 24, No. 2, Cambridge, 1947.

CRESSMAN, L. S. *Petroglyphs of Washington.* University of Oregon Monographs, Studies in Anthropology, No. 2, Eugene, 1937.

——. *Archaeological Researches in the Northern Great Basin.* Carnegie Institution of Washington, Publication 538: XVII-158, 1942.

CUSHING, FRANK H. *Zuni Fetishes.* Second Annual Report of the Bureau of American Ethnology, 1883.

D'AZEVEDO, WARREN, and others. *The Current Status of Anthropological Research in the Great Basin.* Desert Research Institute, University of Nevada, 1964.

DIXON, JOSEPH S. "A Survey of the Desert Bighorn in Death Valley National Monument, Summer, 1938," *California Fish and Game,* Vol. 25 (1939), pp. 72–95.

DRIVER, H. E. *Culture Element Distribution,* VI. *Southern Sierra Nevada.* University of California Anthropological Records, Vol. 1, No. 2, Berkeley and Los Angeles, 1937.

DRUCKER, PHILIP. *Indians of the Northwest Coast.* New York, Natural History Press, 1963.

FARMER, MALCOLM F. "Awatovi Bows," *Plateau* (Museum of Northern Arizona, Flagstaff), Vol. 28, No. 1 (1955).

FLAMAND, G. B. M. *Les Pierres Ecrites (Hadjrat-Mektoubat): Gravures et Inscriptions Rupestres du Nord-Africain.* Paris, Masson et Cie., 1921.

FOLMANN, G. "Lichenometrische Altersbestimmungen an vorchristlichen Steinsetzungen der polynesischen Osterinsel," *Natur-wissenschaften,* (Berlin), Vol. 19 (1961), pp. 627–28.

GEIST, Valerius. "A Consequence of Togetherness," *Natural History Magazine,* (New York), Vol. LXXVI, No. 8, (1967).

GIFFORD, E. W. *Northeastern and Western Yavapai.* University of California Publications in American Archaeology and Ethnology. Vol. 34, No. 4, Berkeley and Los Angeles, 1936.

GRANT, CAMPBELL. *The Rock Painting of the Chumash.* Berkeley, University of California Press, 1965.

——. *Rock Art of the American Indian.* New York, Thomas Y. Crowell Co., 1967.

——. "The Desert Bighorn Rock Drawings of the Coso Range, Inyo County, California," in Desert Bighorn Council Transactions, 1968.

GROSSCUP, G. L. "The Culture History of Lovelock Cave, Nevada," University of California Archaeological Survey (Berkeley), No. 52, 1960.

GRUBER, ABRAHAM. "A Survey of Petroglyphs in Black Canyon," *Southwest Museum Masterkey,* (Los Angeles), Vol. 35, No. 3. (1961).

GUERNSEY, S. J. *Explorations in Northeastern Arizona.* Papers of the Peabody Museum, Vol. 12, No. 1, Cambridge, 1931.

GUERNSEY, S. J. and ALFRED V. KIDDER. *Basketmaker Caves of Northeastern Arizona.* Papers of the Peabody Museum, Vol. 8, No. 2, Cambridge, 1921.

HALL, E. R. *Mammals of Nevada.* Berkeley, University of California Press, 1946.

HALL, R., and K. R. KELSON. *Mammals of North America.* New York, Ronald Press, 1959.

HANSEN, CHARLES G. *Hunting Bighorn Sheep in Nevada.* Las Vegas, State of Fish and Game Commission and the Fraternity of the Desert Bighorn. 1966.

HARRINGTON, M. R. *A Pinto Site at Little Lake, California.* Southwest Museum Papers, No. 17, Los Angeles, 1957.

——. "A Two Purpose Atlatl," *Southwest Museum Masterkey* (Los Angeles), Vol. 33, No. 2 (1959), p. 60.

HAURY, EMIL W. *Painted Cave, Northeastern Arisona.* Amerind Foundation Paper, No. 3, 1945.

HEIZER, ROBERT F. "A Complete Atlatl Dart from Pershing County, Nevada," *New Mexico Anthropologist,* Vol. 2, No. 4 and 5 (1938), pp. 68, 70–71.

——. "An Inquiry into the Status of the Santa Barbara Spear-Thrower," *American Antiquity,* Vol. 4, No. 2 (1938), pp. 137–41.

——. Preliminary Report on the Leonard Rockshelter, Pershing County, Nevada," *American Antiquity,* Vol. 17, No. 2 (1951), pp. 89–98.

HEIZER, ROBERT F., and MARTIN A. BAUMHOFF. *Prehistoric Rock Art of Nevada and Eastern California.* Berkeley, University of California Press, 1962.

HILL, MALCOLM W. "The Atlatl or Throwing Stick. A Recent Study of Atlatls in Use With Darts of Various Sizes," *Tennessee Archaeologist* (Knoxville), Vol. 4, No. 4, (1948) pp. 37–44.

——. "Atlatl Weight Forms," *Tennessee Archaeologist* (Knoxville), Vol. 5, No. 3 (1949).

HUNT, C. B. "Desert Varnish," *Science,* Vol. CXX, No. 3109 (1954), pp. 183–84.

JACKSON, A. T. *Picture Writing of Texas Indians.* Bureau of Research in the Social Sciences, Study No. 27. Austin, University of Texas Press, 1938.

JENNINGS, JESSE D. "Danger Cave," Memoirs of the Society of American Archaeology, No. 14, *American Antiquity,* Vol. 23, No. 2, Part 2, (1957), pp. 85–98.

JENNINGS, JESSE D., and EDWARD NORBECK. "Great Basin Prehistory: A review," *American Antiquity,* Vol. 21 (1955), pp. 1–11.

JEPSEN, W. L. *A Manual of the Flowering Plants of California.* Berkeley, Sather Gate, 1925.

JOHNSTON, F. R. "Art Gallery of Ancient Indians," *Desert Magazine,* Vol. 1, No. 5 (1938).

JOHNSTONE, PHILIP. "Prehistoric Pageantry in Stone," (earliest published description of the Coso Range draw ings), *Touring Topics* (Los Angeles), Vol. 28, No. 11 (1933).

JONES, FRED M., GLENN FLITTNER, and RICHARD GARD. "Report on a Survey of Bighorn Sheep in the Santa Rosa Mountains, Riverside, California," *California Fish and Game* (Sacramento), Vol. 43, No. 3 (1957).

KELLER, JAMES H. *The Atlatl in North America.* Indiana Historical Society Prehistory Research Series, Vol. III, No. 3, Indianapolis, 1955.

KELLEY, J. CHARLES. "Atlatls, Bows and Arrows, Pictographs and the Pecos River Focus," *American Antiquity,* Vol. 16, No. 1 (1950) pp. 71–74.

KIDDER, ALFRED V., and S. J. GUERNSEY. *Archaeological Explorations in Northeastern Arizona.* Bureau of American Ethnology Bulletin, No. 65, Washington, D.C., 1919.

KIRKLAND, FORREST, and W. W. NEWCOMB, JR. *The Rock Art of Texas Indians* Austen, University of Texas Press, 1967.

KROEBER, A. L. *Handbook of the Indians of California.* Bureau of American Ethnology Bulletin, No. 78, Washington, D.C., 1925.

LAMB, SIDNEY M. "Linguistic Prehistory in the Great Basin," *International Journal of American Linguistics,* Vol. 24 (1958), pp. 95—100.

LAUDERMILK, J. D. "On the Origin of Desert Varnish," *American Journal of Science,* (New Haven), Fifth Series, Vol. XXI, No. 121, (1931), pp. 51—66.

LEADABRAND, RUSS. "Treasure Canyon of the Coso Ancients," *Desert Magazine,* Vol. 19, No. 2 (1956).

LEONARD, ZENAS. *Narrative of the Adventures of Zenas Leonard.* University of Oklahoma Press, 1959.

LEOPOLD, STARKER. *Wildlife of Mexico, Game Birds and Mammals.* Berkeley, University of California Press, 1959.

LHOTE, H. *The Search for the Tassili Frescoes.* Trans. by Alan H. Broderick. New York, Dutton, 1959.

LOUD, L. L., and M. R. HARRINGTON. *Lovelock Cave.* University of California Publications in American Archaeology and Ethnology, 251:vii-183, Berkeley, 1929.

MACGOWAN, KENNETH, and JOSEPH A. HESTER, JR. *Early Man in the New World.* New York, Doubleday, 1962.

MALLERY, GARRICK. *Pictographs of the North American Indians.* Fourth Annual Report of the Bureau of American Ethnology, Washington, D.C., 1886.

—— *Picture-Writing of the American Indians.* Tenth Annual Report of the Bureau of American Ethnology, Washington, D.C., 1893.

MARTIN, PAUL S., and others. *Mogollon Cultural Continuity and Change. The Stratigraphic Analysis of Tularosa and Cordova Caves.* Fieldiana: Anthropology, Vol. 40, Chicago Natural History Museum, 1952.

MORRIS, EARL H. *Archaeological Background of Dates in Early Arizona Chronology.* Tre Ring Bulletin, Vol. 2, No. 4, University of Arizona, Tuscon, 1936, pp. 34—36.

——. *Archaeological Studies in the La Plata District, Southwestern Colorado and Northwestern New Mexico.* Carnegie Institution of Washington, Publication 519, 1939.

MORSS, N. *The Ancient Culture of the Fremont River in Utah.* Papers of the Peabody Museum, Vol. 12, No. 3, Cambridge, 1931.

MUIR, JOHN. "The Mountains of California," New York, The Century Co., 1901. Pp. 300—24.

NUTTAL, ZELIA. *The Atlatl or Spear-thrower of the Ancient Mexicans.* Archaeological and Ethnological Papers of the Peabody Museum, Vol. l, No. 3, Cambridge, 1891.

ROBINSON, CYRIL S. and FRED P. CRONEMILLER. "Notes on the Habits of the Desert Bighorn in the San Gabriel Mountains of California," *California Fish and Game,* (Sacramento), Vol. 40, No. 3 (1954).

RUSSO, JOHN P. *The Desert Bighorn Sheep in Arizona, a Research and Management Study.* Arizona Game and Fish Department, Federal Aid Project W-55-R, 1956.

SAYLES, E. B., and ERNST ANTEVS. *The Cochise Culture.* Medallion Papers, No. XXIX. Globe, Arizona, Gila Pueblo, pp. 31-43. 1941.

SCHUMACHER, G. *Deepest Valley—Guide to the Owens Valley and Its Mountain Lakes, Roadsides and Trails.* San Francisco, Sierra Club, 1962.

SETON, E. T. *Lives of the Game Animals.* Vol. 3. New York, Doubleday and Page, 1929.

SHUTLER, RICHARD, JR. *Lost City—Pueblo Grande de Nevada.* Nevada State Museum, Anthropological Papers, No. 5, Carson City, 1961.

SMITH, VERNON. "Sheep Hunting Artists of Black Canyon Walls," *Desert Magazine,* Vol. 7, No. 5 (1944).

SNYDER, C. T., GEORGE HARDMAN, and F. F. ZDENEK. *Pleistocene Lakes in the Great Basin. Miscellaneous Geologic Investigations,* Map 1-416. U.S. Geological Survey, Washington, D.C., 1964.

SPEARS, J. R. *Illustrated Sketches of Death Valley.* Chicago and New York, Rand McNalley, 1892.

STEWARD, JULIAN H. *Petroglyphs of California and Adjoining States.* University of California Publications in American Archaeology and Ethnology, Vol. 24, No. 2, Berkeley, 1929.

—— *Ethnography of the Owens Valley Paiute.* University of California Publications in American Archaeology and Ethnology, Vol. 33, No. 3, Berkeley, 1933.

——. *"Petroglyphs of the United States,"* Annual Report of the Smithsonian Institution, Washington, D.C., 1936.

——. *Basin-Plateau Aboriginal Sociopolitical Groups.* Bureau of American Ethnology Bulletin, No. 120, Washington, D.C., 1938.

——. *Archaeological Reconnaissance of Southern Utah.* Smithsonian Institution Bulletin, No. 128, Washington, D.C., 1941.

——. *The Foundations of Basin-Plateau Shoshonean Society.* Unpublished manuscript, 1968.

STEWART, OMAR C. "Tribal Distributions and Boundaries in the Great Basin," in *The Current Status of Anthropological Research in the Great Basin: 1966.* Desert Research Institute, Science and Humanities Publications, No. 1, Reno, 1966.

TAYLOR, W. E. "Archaeological Collections From the Joy Bay Region, Ungava Peninsula," *The Arctic Circular,* Vol. XV, No. 2, (1963), pp. 24–36.

VON WERLHOF, JAY C. "Rock Art of Owens Valley, California," University of California Archaeological Survey (Berkeley), No. 65, 1965.

WELLES, R. E., and F. B. WELLES. *The Bighorn of Death Valley.* Washington, National Park Service, 1961.

WILLCOX, A. R. *Rock Art of South Africa.* Edinburgh, Nelson, 1963. PP. 64–67.

WORMINGTON, H. M. *Ancient Man in North America.* Denver Museum of Natural History, 1949.

——. *A Reappraisal of the Fremont Culture.* Denver Museum of Natural History Proceedings, No. 1, 1955.

ZBUR, RICHARD T. *A Geophysical Investigation of Indian Wells Valley,* China Lake, California, U.S. Naval Ordnance Test Station, 1963.

INDEX

Airport Lake 93, 135
Aldous, M. C. 128
Altithermal Period 6, 112
Amargosa Range 106
Amargosa River 5
Anasazi 36, 41, 50, 124
Antelope 3, 10, 33, 91
Antevs, Ernst 4
Argus Range 2, 3, 14, 106, 108
   127, 135
Arizona ... 35, 42, 51, 52, 57, 122, 123
   124, 126, 127, 128, 130
Atlatl description of
   efficiency of 50, 52
   arrival in Coso Region 50, 51
   replaced by bow 50, 51
Australia
   Rock Art 29
   Aborigines and use of spear
    thrower 53, 55
Baegert, Johann Jacob 51
Baja California 131
Basketmaker 6, 35, 52, 56, 122
Basketry 78
Baumhoff, Martin A. ... 15, 17, 29, 41
   104, 131
Beschel, Ronald 47, 48
Birchim Spring 95
Bishop 104
Black Canyon 12, 96, 111
Buffalo 33, 34, 39, 42, 114
Carricut, John 14
Carricut Lake 96, 97
Carter, Robert A. 14
Cave Canyon 78
Caves 6, 57, 61, 78, 79, 92, 93
   137, 138
China Lake Basin 4, 5, 12, 44, 45
   91, 137
Coles Spring 92, 93
Colorado Plateau 8, 44
Colorado River 114, 124, 130
Columbia River ... 18, 33, 52, 131, 132
Coronado, Francisco Vasquez 125
Coso Hot Springs 2, 8, 9, 10, 59
   89, 90, 96, 135
Coso Peak 12, 30, 59, 92, 93, 136
Coso Range 16
   geology 135, 136
   Archaeology sites 137, 138

Cushing, F. H. 35
Danger Cave 42
Darwin Wash 10, 91
Death Valley 2, 5, 8, 10, 41, 106
   107, 108, 127, 128, 131
Deer 3, 18, 33, 34, 39, 61, 90, 95
   104, 106, 108
Desert bighorn 3
   range 125, 126
   description 127
   feeding habits 128
   breeding habits 128, 129
   enemies 129
De Soto, Hernando 51
Dogs 18, 29, 42, 72, 91, 96, 104
Driver H. E. 32
Drucker, Philip 34
Eastern Woodland 33
Eskimos 34, 48, 51
Erosion 43, 48
Escalante, Silvestre de 126
Etcheron Valley 59, 76, 90
Eureka Valley 2
Farmer, M. F. 50
Fetish Stones 35
Flamand, G. B. M. 43, 44
Food Gathering Techniques 10
Folmann, Gerhard 48
Fossil Falls 4
Four Corners . 33, 42, 50, 114, 130, 131
French, Dr. Darwin 8
Fremont Culture 124
Geist, Valerius 41, 42
Glottochronology 8, 34, 124
Grapevine Canyon 124
Great Basin ... 2, 8, 14, 17, 29, 30, 33
   42, 49, 50, 104, 106, 108, 112, 124
   126, 130, 135
Great Plains 33, 34, 122
Grosscup, Gordon L. 50, 51, 57
Guernsey, Samuel J. 35, 52
Haiwee Springs 90, 96
Harrington, M. R. 5, 6, 7, 56, 94
Heizer, Robert F. 15, 17, 29, 41
   104, 131
Hill, Malcolm 53
Horse Canyon 73
House Rings 7, 79, 91, 93
Hunt, C. B. 44
Hunting blinds 29, 30, 31, 53, 60
   70, 79, 91, 92, 97

Hunting Magic .. 29, 32, 33, 34, 39, 40
    41, 42, 53, 113, 114, 131
Hunting Techniques 29, 30
    Antelope 10, 91, 113
    Rabbits 10
    Deer 10, 113
    Mt. Sheep ... 10, 22, 30, 31, 32, 42
        53, 79, 113
Idaho 8, 126, 132, 133
Indian Wells Valley 2, 10, 33, 91
Inyo Range 2, 4, 10, 104, 106, 127
Jackson, A. T. 52
Jennings, Jesse D. 42
Johnson, F. R. 14
Johnston, Philip 14
Junction Ranch ..14, 37, 59, 90, 91, 92, 96
Kachina 16
Keeler 104
Kern River 7, 89, 94, 106, 108
Kidder, Alfred 35
Kirkland, F. 36, 52
Kroeber, A. L. 8, 104
Lake Winnemucca 52
Lamb, S. M. 8, 41, 58, 124
Laudermilk, J. D. 44
Leonard Rock Shelter 50
Leonard, Zenas 7
Lhote, Henri 33
Lichen 43, 44, 47, 48, 60
Linguistic Stocks
    Shoshonean 8
    Takic 8
    Numic 8, 41, 58, 114
    Shoshoni-Comanche 8
    Northern Paiute 8
    Ute-Southern Paiute-Chemehuevi .. 8
    Uto-Aztecan 8, 49
Little Lake 2, 5, 6, 7, 8, 10, 55, 56
    89, 94, 104
Loring, Malcolm 132
Louisiana Butte 12, 30, 70, 138
Lovelock Cave 50, 55, 57
Mallory, Garrick 14
Manley Lake 5
Mano 6, 7, 72
Martin, Donald 44, 106
Maturango Peak 127
McCarthy 53
Medicine bag ... 18, 22, 36, 39, 71, 92
    97, 104, 124
Metates (milling stones) ... 6, 7, 30, 70
    72, 77, 79, 91, 92
Mexico 33, 52
Migrations ... 41, 42, 58, 114, 123, 130
Mojave Desert 44, 108
Mojave River 5
Montana 133

Monterey 7
Morss, Noel 124
Mortar 77, 92
Mountain Springs Canyon 95, 127
Muir, John 30, 31, 130
Muddy River 41
Naval Weapons Center 1, 3, 14, 77
    91, 137
Nevada ... 8, 15, 18, 30, 36, 41, 50, 52
    58, 126, 128, 131, 133
Newcomb, W. W. 36, 52
New Mexico 51, 126, 133
Northern Woodland 33
Northwest 33, 34, 41
Obelisk Cave 51
Olancha 2, 10
Oregon 8, 132, 133
Owens Lake 2, 4, 5, 6, 10, 33, 42
    89, 91, 104, 113
Owens River 5, 104
Owens Valley .. 8, 89, 94, 104, 106, 127
Paintings 25, 26, 58, 89, 90, 94
    106, 108, 111, 115, 131, 133
Palaeolithic Rock Art (French and
    Spanish) 29
Panamint Lake 5
Panamint Range 10, 106
Panamint Valley 2, 4, 108
Patina (Desert varnish) 17, 25, 39, 43, 44
    45, 46, 57, 71, 78, 91, 108, 130
Petroglyph Canyon . 39, 59, 70, 71, 106
Pinto Basin 6, 56, 57
Pit-and-groove 16, 17, 22, 58, 95
Pluvial 4, 6, 7, 14, 44, 57, 78, 89
    113
Pottery 7, 11, 50, 78
Pueblo culture 16, 41, 115, 124
Radiocarbon 50
Renegade Canyon 76, 88
Rose Valley 10
Ross Cave 96
Ruby Spring 95
Russo, J. P. 127
Saline Range 106
Saline Valley 2, 8, 10
Salmon 33, 34
Sand Tanks 12
San Joaquin Valley .. 7, 11, 89, 106, 108
San Juan River 52, 114, 124
Sayles, E. B. 4
Searles Lake 4, 5, 6
Seton, Ernest Thompson 126, 128
Shaman 39, 40, 115
Sheep Canyon 70, 76
Sheep cult theory ... 34, 39, 40, 41, 42
Shield patterns .. 18, 22, 39, 42, 60, 61
    79, 89, 91, 96, 97, 106, 124
Shutler, R. 41

Sierra Nevada .. 2, 4, 7, 10, 18, 55, 108
    111, 113, 114, 122, 127, 131
Silver Peak 30, 136
Smith, Vernon 14
Southwest 33, 42, 48, 50, 51
    123, 126, 130
Stahl Site 56, 57, 94
Stahl, Willy 7
Steward, Julian H. .. 8, 9, 14, 15, 32, 33
    104, 106, 124
Strong, Emory 33, 52
Styles
    Coso Naturalistic 16, 17, 18, 24
    Coso Stylized 16, 17, 18, 24
    Coso Abstract 16, 17, 18, 24
    Great Basin Abstract 17, 29, 89
        94, 106, 111, 115
    Pit-and-groove 16, 17, 22, 24, 58, 95
Sugar Loaf Mt. 6
Superimposition 56
Taylor, W. E. 48
Tehachapi Mountains 94, 108, 111
Texas ..8, 18, 36, 41, 51, 52, 126, 131, 133
Tracks 91, 94
Trans-Pecos 91, 94
Tribes
    Apache 133
    Aztec 8, 115
    Chemehuevi 8, 106
    Chumash 7, 108
    Gabrielino 8
    Hopi 8, 124
    Kawaiisu 89, 94, 106, 108, 111
    Navajo 16, 115
    Paiute, Northern 8
    Paiute, Owens Valley 8, 32, 104, 108
    Paiute, Southern 8, 36, 41
    Pima 8
    Serrano 8
    Tubatulabal 89, 108, 111
    Western Shoshoni ... 6, 8, 9, 11, 32
        94, 106, 108
    Yokuts 11, 108
    Yurok 34
    Zuni 35
Trona 5
Tularosa Cave 51
Upper Centennial Flat 92
Upper Centennial Spring 92
Utah ... 8, 42, 52, 114, 124, 126, 130, 131
Valley of Fire 124
Ventana Cave 51
Virgin River 41, 124
von Werlhof, Jay C. 17, 104
Walker, Joseph 7
Walker Pass 90, 94, 106
Welles, Ralph and Florence ... 127, 128
    129

White Mountains 104
Wild Horse Mesa ... 12, 30, 70, 76, 77
Wilcox, S. R. 43
Wilson Canyon 93, 127
Wingate Pass 5
Wisconsin glaciation 44
Wormington, H. M. 124
Wyoming ... 8, 41, 126, 131, 132, 133